Practice in the B Mathema

Contents

Published by Collins Educational
An imprint of HarperCollins*Publishers* Ltd
77-85 Fulham Palace Road
London W6 8JB

www.CollinsEducation.com
On-line support for schools and colleges

© Derek Newton and David Smith 2003
First published 1978

This edition published in 2003

16 15 14 13 12

ISBN-13 978-0-00-717719-6

ISBN-10 0-00-717719-4

The authors assert the moral right to be identified
as the authors of this work.

British Library Cataloguing in Publication Data
A catalogue record for this book is available from
the British Library.

Printed in China

Groups

How many?

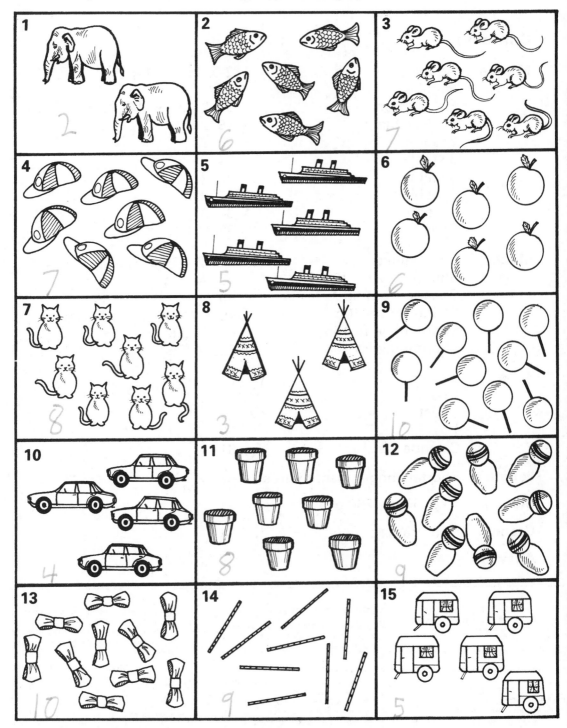

Addition

How many altogether?

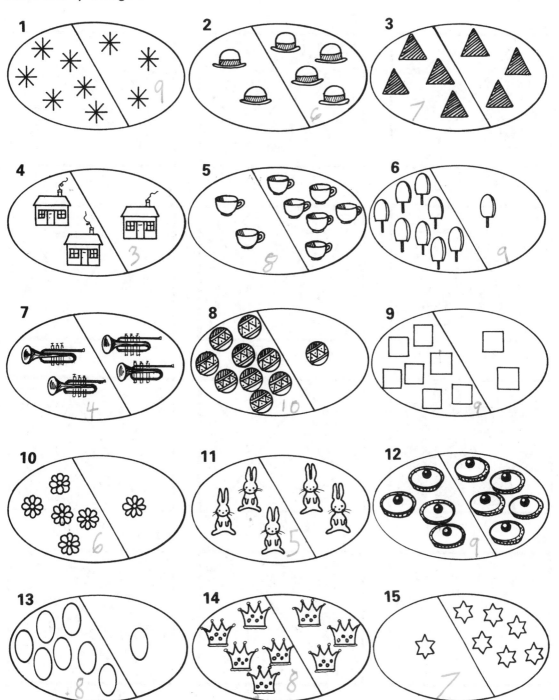

Addition

Copy and complete.

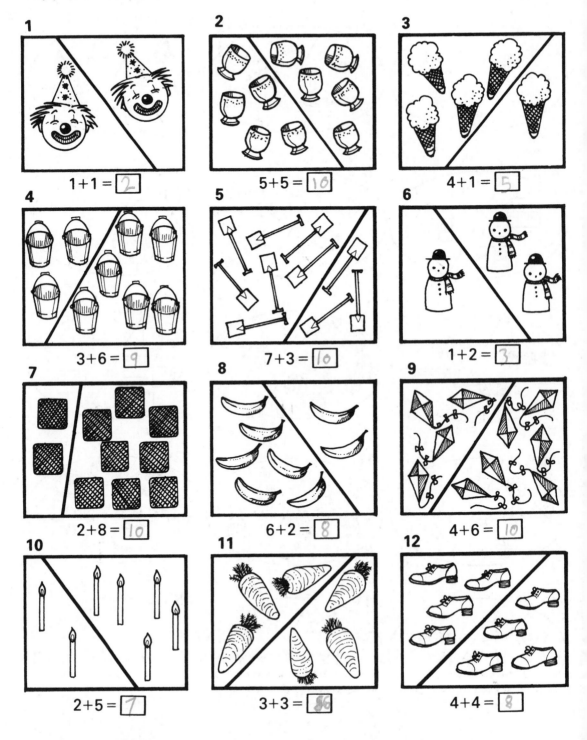

1

$1+1=\boxed{2}$

2

$5+5=\boxed{10}$

3

$4+1=\boxed{5}$

4

$3+6=\boxed{9}$

5

$7+3=\boxed{10}$

6

$1+2=\boxed{3}$

7

$2+8=\boxed{10}$

8

$6+2=\boxed{8}$

9

$4+6=\boxed{10}$

10

$2+5=\boxed{7}$

11

$3+3=\boxed{6}$

12

$4+4=\boxed{8}$

Addition

Write your own number sentences.

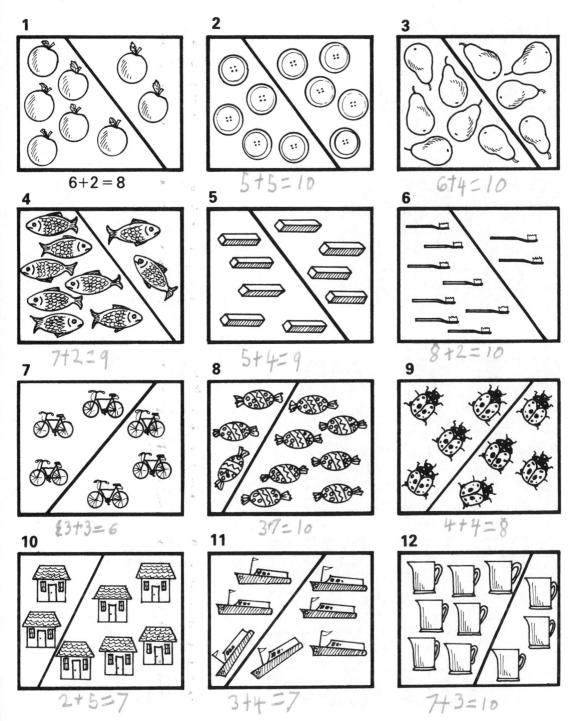

1
$6 + 2 = 8$

2
$5 + 5 = 10$

3
$6 + 4 = 10$

4
$7 + 2 = 9$

5
$5 + 4 = 9$

6
$8 + 2 = 10$

7
$3 + 3 = 6$

8
$3 + 7 = 10$

9
$4 + 4 = 8$

10
$2 + 5 = 7$

11
$3 + 4 = 7$

12
$7 + 3 = 10$

Number families

A Write the 5 family.

$5 + 0 = 5$
$4 + 1 = 5$
$3 + 2 = 5$
$2 + 3 = 5$
$1 + 4 = 5$
$0 + 5 = 5$

B Write the 6 family.

$6 + 0 = 6$
$5 + 1 = 6$
$4 + 2 = 6$
$3 + 3 = 6$
$2 + 4 = 6$
$1 + 5 = 6$
$0 + 6 = 6$

C Write the 7 family.

$7 + 0 = 7$
$6 + 1 = 7$
$5 + 2 = 7$
$4 + 3 = 7$
$3 + 4 = 7$
$2 + 5 = 7$
$1 + 6 = 7$
$0 + 7 = 7$

D Write the 8 family.

$8 + 0 = 8$
$7 + 1 = 8$
$6 + 2 = 8$
$5 + 3 = 8$
$4 + 4 = 8$
$3 + 5 = 8$
$2 + 6 = 8$
$1 + 7 = 8$
$0 + 8 = 8$

More number families

A   The 9 family

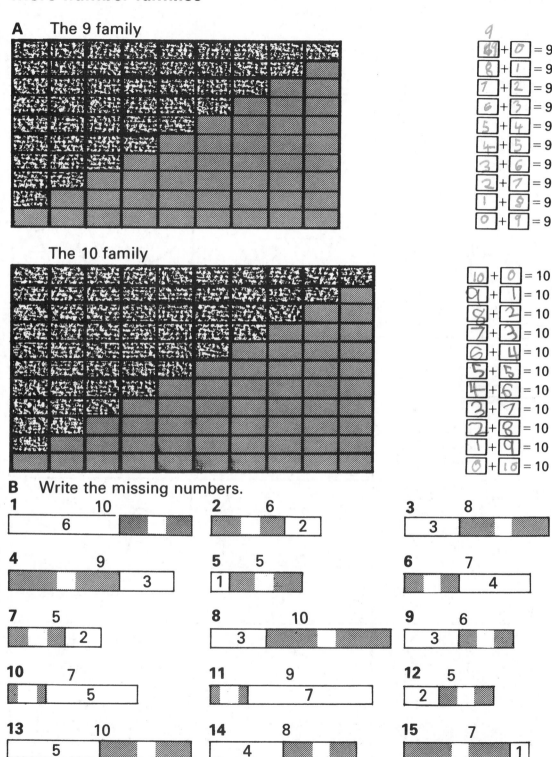

9

9	+ 0	= 9
8	+ 1	= 9
7	+ 2	= 9
6	+ 3	= 9
5	+ 4	= 9
4	+ 5	= 9
3	+ 6	= 9
2	+ 7	= 9
1	+ 8	= 9
0	+ 9	= 9

The 10 family

10	+ 0	= 10
9	+ 1	= 10
8	+ 2	= 10
7	+ 3	= 10
6	+ 4	= 10
5	+ 5	= 10
4	+ 6	= 10
3	+ 7	= 10
2	+ 8	= 10
1	+ 9	= 10
0	+ 10	= 10

B   Write the missing numbers.

1   10   — 6 —

2   6   — 2

3   8   — 3 —

4   9   — 3

5   5   1 —

6   7   — 4

7   5   — 2

8   10   3 —

9   6   3 —

10   7   — 5

11   9   — 7

12   5   2 —

13   10   5 —

14   8   4 —

15   7   — 1

Subtraction

How many left?

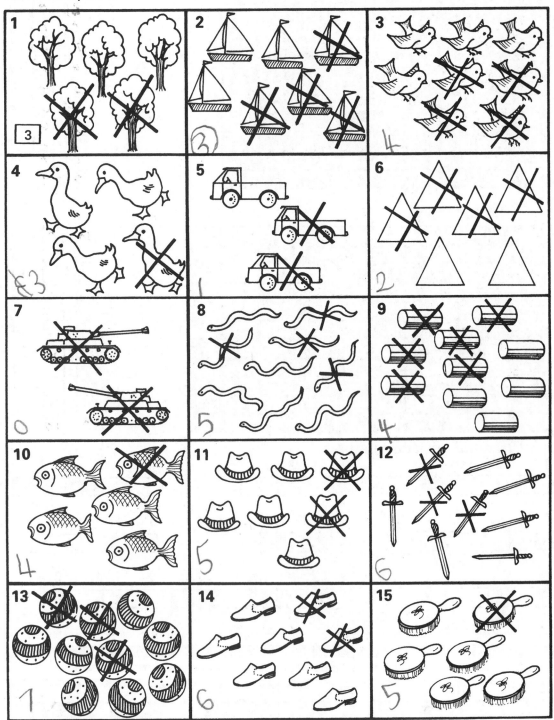

Subtraction

Complete the number sentences.

1 $9-4=\boxed{5}$

2 $10-3=\boxed{6}$

3 $7-2=\boxed{5}$

4 $8-6=\boxed{2}$

5 $4-3=\boxed{1}$

6 $6-6=\boxed{0}$

7 $5-4=\boxed{1}$

8 $3-1=\boxed{2}$

9 $2-1=\boxed{1}$

10 $10-6=\boxed{4}$

11 $9-5=\boxed{4}$

12 $7-4=\boxed{3}$

Subtraction

Write your own number sentences.

1. $7-3=4$
2. $5-5$, $10-5=5$
3. $9-3=6$
4. $8-3=5$
5. $4-2=2$
6. $3-2=1$
7. $8-2=6$
8. $2-1=1$
9. $9-2=7$
10. $8-7=1$
11. $5-3=2$
12. $7-1=6$

Addition — number lines

A

Use the number line to add 2.

$3+2=\boxed{5}$ $7+2=\boxed{9}$ $1+2=\boxed{3}$ $8+2=\boxed{10}$

$4+2=\boxed{6}$ $6+2=\boxed{8}$ $5+2=\boxed{7}$ $2+2=\boxed{4}$

B

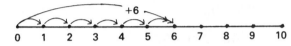

Use the number line to add 6.

$0+6=\boxed{6}$ $2+6=\boxed{8}$ $4+6=\boxed{10}$ $3+6=\boxed{9}$

$1+6=\boxed{7}$

C

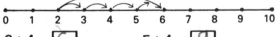

Use the number line to add 3.

$1+3=\boxed{4}$ $4+3=\boxed{7}$ $6+3=\boxed{9}$ $3+3=\boxed{6}$

$0+3=\boxed{3}$ $2+3=\boxed{5}$ $5+3=\boxed{8}$ $7+3=\boxed{10}$

D

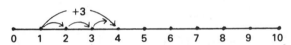

$2+4=\boxed{6}$ $5+4=\boxed{9}$ $1+4=\boxed{5}$ $6+4=\boxed{10}$

$3+4=\boxed{7}$ $0+4=\boxed{4}$ $4+4=\boxed{8}$

E

$5+5=\boxed{10}$ $0+5=\boxed{5}$ $3+5=\boxed{8}$ $2+5=\boxed{7}$

$4+5=\boxed{9}$ $1+5=\boxed{6}$

Subtraction — number lines

A

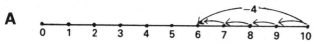

Use the number line to subtract 4.

$10-4=\boxed{6}$ $\quad$ $4-4=\boxed{0}$ $\quad$ $7-4=\boxed{3}$ $\quad$ $5-4=\boxed{1}$ $\quad$ $9-4=\boxed{5}$

$6-4=\boxed{22}$ $\quad$ $8-4=\boxed{4}$

B

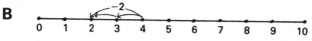

Use the number line to subtract 2.

$4-2=\boxed{22}$ $\quad$ $7-2=\boxed{5}$ $\quad$ $10-2=\boxed{8}$ $\quad$ $3-2=\boxed{1}$ $\quad$ $5-2=\boxed{3}$

$9-2=\boxed{7}$ $\quad$ $2-2=\boxed{0}$ $\quad$ $6-2=\boxed{4}$ $\quad$ $8-2=\boxed{56}$

C

$10-6=\boxed{4}$ $\quad$ $7-6=\boxed{1}$ $\quad$ $9-6=\boxed{3}$ $\quad$ $6-6=\boxed{0}$ $\quad$ $8-6=\boxed{2}$

D

$5-5=\boxed{0}$ $\quad$ $7-5=\boxed{2}$ $\quad$ $9-5=\boxed{4}$ $\quad$ $6-5=\boxed{1}$ $\quad$ $8-5=\boxed{3}$

$10-5=\boxed{5}$

E

$5-3=\boxed{2}$ $\quad$ $4-3=\boxed{1}$ $\quad$ $6-3=\boxed{3}$ $\quad$ $9-3=\boxed{6}$ $\quad$ $3-3=\boxed{0}$

$10-3=\boxed{7}$ $\quad$ $8-3=\boxed{5}$ $\quad$ $7-3=\boxed{4}$

F

$5-1=\boxed{4}$ $\quad$ $7-1=\boxed{6}$ $\quad$ $2-1=\boxed{1}$ $\quad$ $8-1=\boxed{7}$ $\quad$ $4-1=\boxed{3}$

$10-1=\boxed{9}$ $\quad$ $6-1=\boxed{5}$ $\quad$ $1-1=\boxed{0}$ $\quad$ $9-1=\boxed{8}$ $\quad$ $3-1=\boxed{2}$

More and less than

Use the number strip.

A

| 1 | 2 | 3 | 4 | 5 | 6 | 7 | 8 | 9 | 10 |

4 more than 5 = [9]   9 less than 10 = [1]   3 more than 5 = [8]
7 more than 3 = [10]   2 less than 7 = [5]   8 less than 9 = [1]
5 more than 4 = [9]   5 less than 8 = [3]   1 more than 4 = [5]
9 more than 1 = [10]   3 less than 6 = [3]   2 less than 3 = [1]
6 more than 2 = [8]   7 less than 9 = [2]   6 less than 10 = [4]
2 more than 7 = [9]   4 less than 9 = [5]   7 more than 1 = [8]
1 more than 8 = [9]   8 less than 10 = [2]   4 less than 8 = [4]
3 more than 6 = [9]   1 less than 5 = [4]   9 less than 9 = [0]
8 more than 2 = [10]   6 less than 6 = [0]   5 more than 2 = [7]

B   Use the signs > and <

8 > 1	4 8	5 4
1 < 6	1 1	6 8
3 < 5	4 2	3 6
4 < 5	3 9	2 6
2 < 9	2 3	1 3
10 > 2	9 7	7 1
3 < 9	1 10	9 7
5 < 9	8 5	7 2
9 > 8	5 2	3 7
7 > 4	6 10	10 5
6 > 4	10 6	2 1
5 < 10	8 3	4 8

>

C   Complete each of the following with one number of your own.

5 > [0]   1 > [0]   2 > [1]   4 < [80]
3 > [1]   6 < [100]   7 > [5]   8 > [1]
10 > [6]   9 > [1]   3 < [800]   1 < [9]
4 > [3]   2 < [200]   6 > [1]   8 < [100]

Using the equaliser

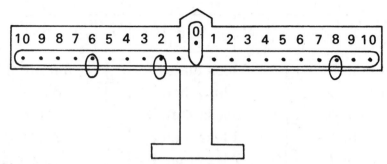

A Use the equaliser to answer.

6+[3] = (9)   3+2 = [5]   5+[5] = 10   5+[2] = 7

[2]+4 = 6   4+[4] = 8   7+2 = [9]   [7]+2 = 9

5+3 = [8]   [8]+1 = 9   [2]+6 = 8   3+[0] = 3

2+[2] = 4   8+2 = [10]   3+[2] = 10   3+4 = [7]

[1]+6 = 7   4+4 = [8]   3+3 = [6]   [0]+8 = 8

6+4 = [10]   1+[4] = 5   2+[4] = 6   8+[2] = 10

B

6+[3]=4+5   [3]+1=2+2

2+5=[3]+4   5+5=[6]+4

3+7=8+[2]   1+[8]=7+2

4+[4]=5+3   5+2=[4]+3

[2]+3=1+4   [8]+2=1+9

[5]+1=3+3   2+4=4+[2]

C

4+2+2=5+[3]   1+[3]+1=3+2

3+4=2+3+[2]   6+3=2+4+[3]

6+2+1=3+2+1+[3]   [4]+2=1+1+4

[5]+2+1=6+2   8+2=4+[4]+2

4+[4]+2=7+3   3+1=1+2+[1]

2+2+2=1+[5]   3+2+3=2+[6]

3+3+[3]=4+5   7+2+1=5+[5]

6+0=3+1+[2]   [5]+4=2+3+4

1+4=2+1+[2]   2+5=3+3+[1]

6+1+[0]=3+4   6+1+[3]=2+5+3

Addition — number ladder

Use the number ladder to add.

Number ladder (vertical, top to bottom): 20, 19, 18, 17, 16, 15, 14, 13, 12, 11, 10, 9, 8, 7, 6, 5, 4, 3, 2, 1, 0

+4 (arrows pointing up along ladder near 9–12)

A
$9+4 = \boxed{13}$ $16+4 = \boxed{20}$ $7+4 = \boxed{11}$ $11+4 = \boxed{15}$
$15+4 = \boxed{19}$ $10+4 = \boxed{14}$ $13+4 = \boxed{17}$ 7 $12+4 = \boxed{16}$
$14+4 = \boxed{18}$ $8+4 = \boxed{12}$ $6+4 = \boxed{10}$

B • $8+7 = \boxed{14}$ 13 $13+7 = \boxed{20}$ $11+7 = \boxed{18}$ $7+7 = \boxed{14}$
$12+7 = \boxed{19}$ $9+7 = \boxed{16}$ $10+7 = \boxed{17}$ $6+7 = \boxed{13}$

C $13+6 = \boxed{19}$ $9+6 = \boxed{15}$ $11+6 = \boxed{17}$ $14+6 = \boxed{20}$
$7+6 = \boxed{13}$ $12+6 = \boxed{18}$ $8+6 = \boxed{14}$ $10+6 = \boxed{16}$

D $12+8 = \boxed{20}$ $7+8 = \boxed{15}$ $10+8 = \boxed{18}$ $9+8 = \boxed{17}$
$11+8 = \boxed{19}$ $5+8 = \boxed{13}$ $8+8 = \boxed{16}$ • $6+8 = \boxed{13}$ 14

E $11+9 = \boxed{20}$0 $9+9 = \boxed{18}$ $10+9 = \boxed{19}$ $7+9 = \boxed{16}$
$8+9 = \boxed{17}$ $6+9 = \boxed{15}$ $4+9 = \boxed{13}$ $3+9 = \boxed{12}$

F $15+5 = \boxed{20}$0 $8+5 = \boxed{13}$ $12+5 = \boxed{17}$ $14+5 = \boxed{19}$
$9+5 = \boxed{14}$ $7+5 = \boxed{12}$ $11+5 = \boxed{16}$ $13+5 = \boxed{18}$
$12+5 = \boxed{17}$ $6+5 = \boxed{11}$

G $13+3 = \boxed{16}$ $16+3 = \boxed{19}$ $8+3 = \boxed{11}$ $17+3 = \boxed{20}$
$10+3 = \boxed{13}$ $15+3 = \boxed{18}$ $12+3 = \boxed{15}$ $9+3 = \boxed{12}$
$11+3 = \boxed{14}$ $7+3 = \boxed{10}$ $14+3 = \boxed{17}$

H $10+10 = \boxed{20}$ $4+10 = \boxed{14}$ $8+10 = \boxed{18}$ $6+10 = \boxed{16}$
$5+10 = \boxed{15}$ $7+10 = \boxed{17}$ $2+10 = \boxed{12}$ $1+10 = \boxed{11}$
$9+10 = \boxed{19}$ $3+10 = \boxed{13}$

I $18+2 = \boxed{20}$ $7+2 = \boxed{9}$ $16+2 = \boxed{18}$ $9+2 = \boxed{11}$
$17+2 = \boxed{19}$ $14+2 = \boxed{16}$ $10+2 = \boxed{12}$ $13+2 = \boxed{15}$
$11+2 = \boxed{13}$ $15+2 = \boxed{17}$ $8+2 = \boxed{10}$

Subtraction — number ladder

Use the number ladder to subtract.

Ladder (top to bottom): 20, 19, 18, 17, 16, 15, 14, 13, 12, 11, 10, 9, 8, 7, 6, 5, 4, 3, 2, 1, 0

-5

A
$12-5=6$ $\qquad$ $19-5=14$ $\qquad$ $13-5=8$ $\qquad$ $20-5=15$
$10-5=5$ $\qquad$ $14-5=9$ $\qquad$ $16-5=11$ $\qquad$ $18-5=13$
$11-5=14$ $\qquad$ $15-5=10$ $\qquad$ $17-5=13$

B
$10-9=1$ $\qquad$ $18-9=9$ $\qquad$ $16-9=7$ $\qquad$ $12-9=4$
$19-9=10$ $\qquad$ $20-9=11$ $\qquad$ $14-9=9$ $\qquad$ $15-9=6$
$13-9=4$ $\qquad$ $17-9=8$ $\qquad$ $11-9=2$

C
$11-6=6$ $\qquad$ $18-6=12$ $\qquad$ $20-6=5$ $\qquad$ $13-6=7$
$12-6=7$ $\qquad$ $19-6=13$ $\qquad$ $16-6=10$ $\qquad$ $14-6=8$
$17-6=11$ $\qquad$ $10-6=4$ $\qquad$ $15-6=9$

D
$13-7=6$ $\qquad$ $20-7=16$ $\qquad$ $10-7=3$ $\qquad$ $18-7=11$
$15-7=8$ $\qquad$ $16-7=9$ $\qquad$ $12-7=5$ $\qquad$ $17-7=10$
$19-7=12$ $\qquad$ $14-7=7$ $\qquad$ $11-7=4$

E
$10-4=6$ $\qquad$ $17-4=13$ $\qquad$ $12-4=8$ $\qquad$ $18-4=14$
$19-4=15$ $\qquad$ $14-4=10$ $\qquad$ $11-4=7$ $\qquad$ $16-4=12$
$13-4=9$ $\qquad$ $20-4=16$ $\qquad$ $15-4=11$

F
$13-8=5$ $\qquad$ $17-8=9$ $\qquad$ $12-8=4$ $\qquad$ $10-8=2$
$20-8=12$ $\qquad$ $18-8=10$ $\qquad$ $16-8=8$ $\qquad$ $14-8=6$
$11-8=3$ $\qquad$ $19-8=11$ $\qquad$ $15-8=7$

G
$12-10=2$ $\qquad$ $15-10=5$ $\qquad$ $10-10=0$ $\qquad$ $20-10=10$
$17-10=7$ $\qquad$ $13-10=3$ $\qquad$ $16-10=6$ $\qquad$ $19-10=9$
$11-10=1$ $\qquad$ $18-10=8$ $\qquad$ $14-10=4$

H
$20-3=17$ $\qquad$ $10-3=7$ $\qquad$ $13-3=10$ $\qquad$ $17-3=14$
$19-3=16$ $\qquad$ $12-3=11$ $\qquad$ $16-3=13$ $\qquad$ $18-3=15$
$14-3=11$ $\qquad$ $11-3=9$ $\qquad$ $15-3=12$

Addition and subtraction — mapping

1	2	3	4	5	6	7	8	9	10	11	12	13	14	15	16	17	18	19	20

Use the number strip to solve these.

1

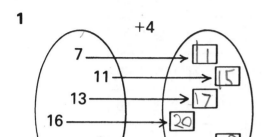

+4

7 → 11
11 → 15
13 → 17
16 → 20
9 → 13
8 → 12

2

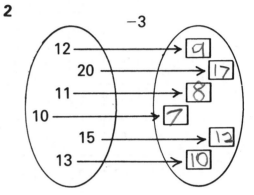

−3

12 → 9
20 → 17
11 → 8
10 → 7
15 → 12
13 → 10

3

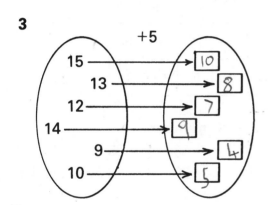

+5

15 → 10
13 → 8
12 → 7
14 → 9
9 → 4
10 → 5

4

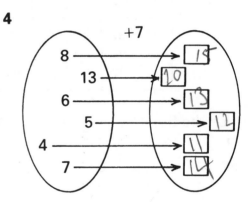

+7

8 → 15
13 → 10
6 → 13
5 → 12
4 → 11
7 → 14

5

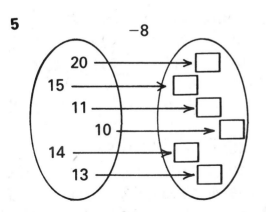

−8

20 → □
15 → □
11 → □
10 → □
14 → □
13 → □

6

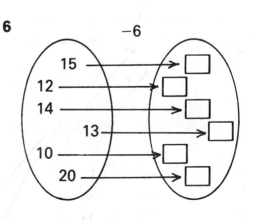

−6

15 → □
12 → □
14 → □
13 → □
10 → □
20 → □

The hundred square — tens

1	2	3	4	5	6	7	8	9	10
11	12	13	14	15	16	17	18	19	20
21	22	23	24	25	26	27	28	29	30
31	32	33	34	35	36	37	38	39	40
41	42	43	44	45	46	47	48	49	50
51	52	53	54	55	56	57	58	59	60
61	62	63	64	65	66	67	68	69	70
71	72	73	74	75	76	77	78	79	80
81	82	83	84	85	86	87	88	89	90
91	92	93	94	95	96	97	98	99	100

A Use the hundred square to add 10 to each number.

25 35   34 44   47 57   22 32   51 61   60 70   85 95   37 47
56 66   78 88   39 49   28 38   33 43   59 69   16 26   42 52

B Use the hundred square to subtract 10 from each number.

41 31   63 53   29 19   54 44   88 78   17 7   52 42   24 14
36 46   69 59   75 65   20 10   14 4   96 86   81 71   72 62

C Complete by adding 10 each time.

1 13, 23, 33, 43, 53, 63, 73, 83, 93
2 45, 55, 65, 75, 85, 95
3 7, 17, 27, 37, 47, 57, 67, 77, 87,
4 12, 22, 32, 42, 52, 62, 72, 82, 92
5 8, 18, 28, 38, 48, 58, 68, 78, 88, 98
6 36, 46, 56, 66, 76, 86, 96
7 24, 34, 44, 54, 64, 74, 84, 94
8 9, 19, 29, 39, 49, 59, 69, 79, 89, 99

The abacus — tens and ones

tens	ones
•	•
•	•
•	•
•	
4	3

$43 \longrightarrow$ 4 tens and 3 ones

A Write out the value on each abacus.

tens	ones
2	6

tens	ones
4	5

tens	ones
1	4

tens	ones
7	1

tens	ones
5	8

tens	ones
4	0

tens	ones
5	2

tens	ones
3	8

tens	ones
9	7

tens	ones
6	3

tens	ones
8	3

tens	ones
0	9

B Draw abaci to show the following numbers.

59   72   41   80   63   44   68   95   36   67

C Write down how many tens in each of these numbers.

27   74   68   43   81   32   16   54   90

More tens and ones

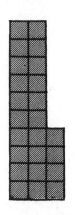

24 ——→ 2 tens and 4 ones

A Write the value of each of these.

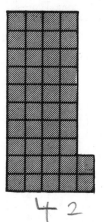 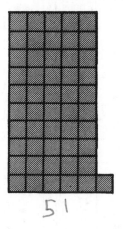 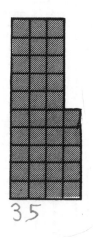 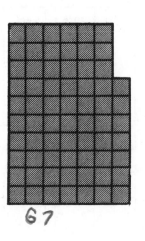

42   51   35   67

B Use squared paper to record these values.

29   17   31   48   56   74   60   85   93   42

C Sort these numbers into tens and ones.

53 ——→ 5 tens and 3 ones

11   67   33   26   42   38   55   64

79   68   92   60   54   23   15   36

87   72   50   41

Addition and subtraction — tens and ones

A

23 + 3 = 26

Use bundles or rods to add.

42+5 = ☐	61+ 6 = ☐	51+38 = ☐	66+22 = ☐
36+3 = ☐	5+21 = ☐	12+57 = ☐	54+34 = ☐
28+1 = ☐	75+ 4 = ☐	70+29 = ☐	28+61 = ☐
53+6 = ☐	98+ 1 = ☐	33+44 = ☐	47+51 = ☐
14+4 = ☐	87+ 2 = ☐	75+23 = ☐	89+10 = ☐

B

36 – 2 = 34

Use bundles or rods to subtract.

29−6 = ☐	48−4 = ☐	37−24 = ☐	43−21 = ☐
34−3 = ☐	64−2 = ☐	48−32 = ☐	47−34 = ☐
28−5 = ☐	35−3 = ☐	29−16 = ☐	54−33 = ☐
46−4 = ☐	27−5 = ☐	36−25 = ☐	29−17 = ☐
38−6 = ☐	36−4 = ☐	42−21 = ☐	66−43 = ☐
55−2 = ☐	26−5 = ☐	35−25 = ☐	48−34 = ☐
37−3 = ☐	19−4 = ☐	84−22 = ☐	29−28 = ☐

C Write down how many are needed to make each of these numbers up to the next ten.

41	35	63	54	89	72
26	18	97	50		

Groups of two

A Complete the number sentences.

$1 \times 2 = 2$

$6 \times 2 = \square$

$12 \times 2 = \square$

$4 \times 2 = \square$

$7 \times 2 = \square$

$10 \times 2 = \square$

$5 \times 2 = \square$

$8 \times 2 = \square$

$11 \times 2 = \square$

$2 \times 2 = \square$

$9 \times 2 = \square$

$3 \times 2 = \square$

B Copy and complete

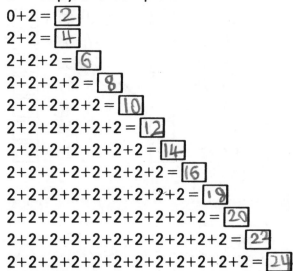

$0 + 2 = \boxed{2}$

$2 + 2 = \boxed{4}$

$2 + 2 + 2 = \boxed{6}$

$2 + 2 + 2 + 2 = \boxed{8}$

$2 + 2 + 2 + 2 + 2 = \boxed{10}$

$2 + 2 + 2 + 2 + 2 + 2 = \boxed{12}$

$2 + 2 + 2 + 2 + 2 + 2 + 2 = \boxed{14}$

$2 + 2 + 2 + 2 + 2 + 2 + 2 + 2 = \boxed{16}$

$2 + 2 + 2 + 2 + 2 + 2 + 2 + 2 + 2 = \boxed{18}$

$2 + 2 + 2 + 2 + 2 + 2 + 2 + 2 + 2 + 2 = \boxed{20}$

$2 + 2 + 2 + 2 + 2 + 2 + 2 + 2 + 2 + 2 + 2 = \boxed{22}$

$2 + 2 + 2 + 2 + 2 + 2 + 2 + 2 + 2 + 2 + 2 + 2 = \boxed{24}$

$1 \times 2 = \boxed{2}$

$2 \times 2 = \boxed{4}$

$3 \times 2 = \boxed{6}$

$4 \times 2 = \boxed{8}$

$5 \times 2 = \boxed{10}$

$6 \times 2 = \boxed{12}$

$7 \times 2 = \boxed{14}$

$8 \times 2 = \boxed{16}$

$9 \times 2 = \boxed{18}$

$10 \times 2 = \boxed{20}$

$11 \times 2 = \boxed{22}$

$12 \times 2 = \boxed{24}$

Groups of two

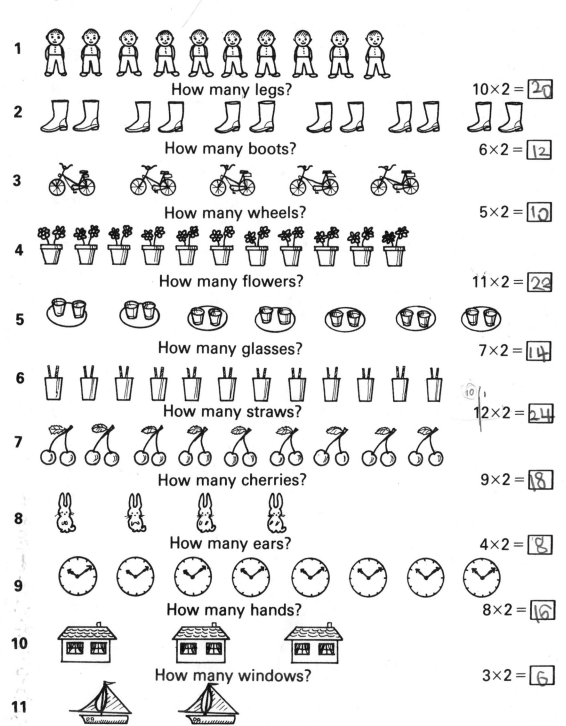

1 How many legs? $10 \times 2 = \boxed{20}$

2 How many boots? $6 \times 2 = \boxed{12}$

3 How many wheels? $5 \times 2 = \boxed{10}$

4 How many flowers? $11 \times 2 = \boxed{22}$

5 How many glasses? $7 \times 2 = \boxed{14}$

6 How many straws? $12 \times 2 = \boxed{24}$

7 How many cherries? $9 \times 2 = \boxed{18}$

8 How many ears? $4 \times 2 = \boxed{8}$

9 How many hands? $8 \times 2 = \boxed{16}$

10 How many windows? $3 \times 2 = \boxed{6}$

11 How many sails? $2 \times 2 = \boxed{4}$

Groups of three

A Complete the number sentences.

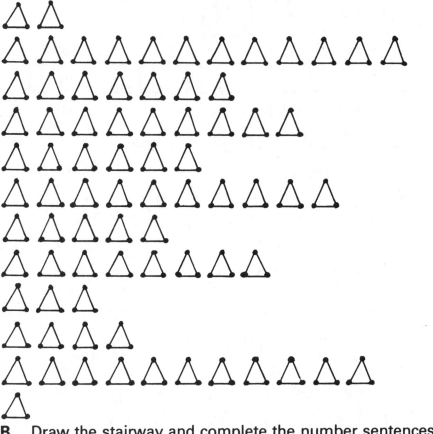

$2 \times 3 = \boxed{6}$ 6

$12 \times 3 = \boxed{36}$ 3

$7 \times 3 = \boxed{21}$ 1

$9 \times 3 = \boxed{27}$ 7

$6 \times 3 = \boxed{18}$

$10 \times 3 = \boxed{30}$ 0

$5 \times 3 = \boxed{15}$

$8 \times 3 = \boxed{24}$ 4

$3 \times 3 = \boxed{9}$

$4 \times 3 = \boxed{12}$

$11 \times 3 = \boxed{33}$ 3

$1 \times 3 = \boxed{3}$

B Draw the stairway and complete the number sentences.

3											
3	3										
3	3	3									
3	3	3	3								
3	3	3	3	3							
3	3	3	3	3	3						
3	3	3	3	3	3	3					
3	3	3	3	3	3	3	3				
3	3	3	3	3	3	3	3	3			
3	3	3	3	3	3	3	3	3	3		
3	3	3	3	3	3	3	3	3	3	3	
3	3	3	3	3	3	3	3	3	3	3	3

$1 \times 3 = \boxed{3}$

$2 \times 3 = \boxed{6}$ 6

$3 \times 3 = \boxed{9}$

$4 \times 3 = \boxed{12}$ 2

$5 \times 3 = \boxed{1}$ 5

$6 \times 3 = \boxed{1}$

$7 \times 3 = \boxed{2}$

$8 \times 3 = \boxed{2}$

$9 \times 3 = \boxed{2}$

$10 \times 3 = \boxed{3}$

$11 \times 3 = \boxed{3}$

$12 \times 3 = \boxed{3}$

Groups of three

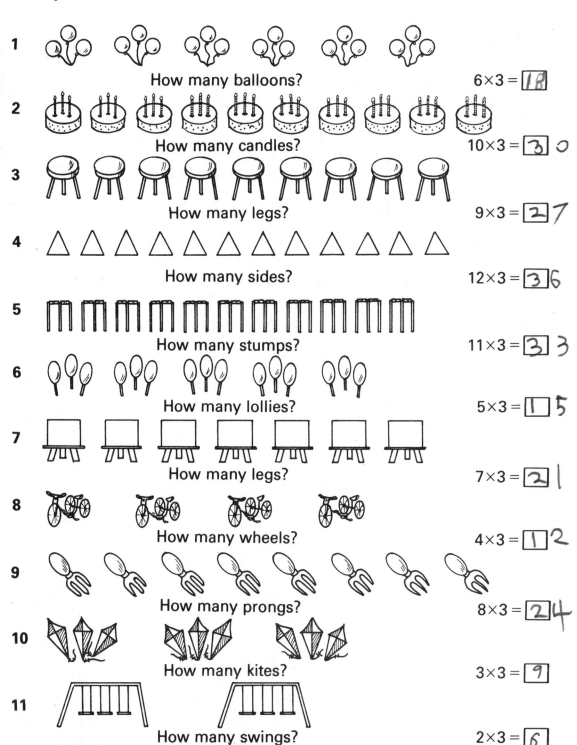

1 How many balloons? $6 \times 3 = 18$

2 How many candles? $10 \times 3 = 30$

3 How many legs? $9 \times 3 = 27$

4 How many sides? $12 \times 3 = 36$

5 How many stumps? $11 \times 3 = 33$

6 How many lollies? $5 \times 3 = 15$

7 How many legs? $7 \times 3 = 21$

8 How many wheels? $4 \times 3 = 12$

9 How many prongs? $8 \times 3 = 24$

10 How many kites? $3 \times 3 = 9$

11 How many swings? $2 \times 3 = 6$

Groups of four

A   Complete the number sentences.

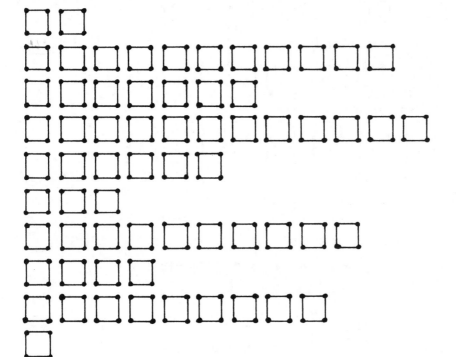

$2\times4=$ 8

$11\times4=$ 44

$7\times4=$ 28

$12\times4=$ 48

$6\times4=$ 24

$3\times4=$ 12

$10\times4=$ 40

$4\times4=$ 16

$9\times4=$ 36

$1\times4=$ 4

$5\times4=$ 20

$8\times4=$ 32

B   Complete the number sentences.

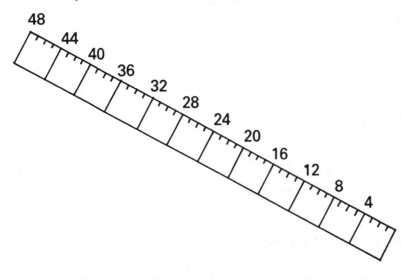

$1\times4=$ 4

$2\times4=$ 8

$3\times4=$ 12

$4\times4=$ 16

$5\times4=$ 20

$6\times4=$ 24

$7\times4=$ 28

$8\times4=$ 32

$9\times4=$ 36

$10\times4=$ 40

$11\times4=$ 44

$12\times4=$ 48

Groups of four

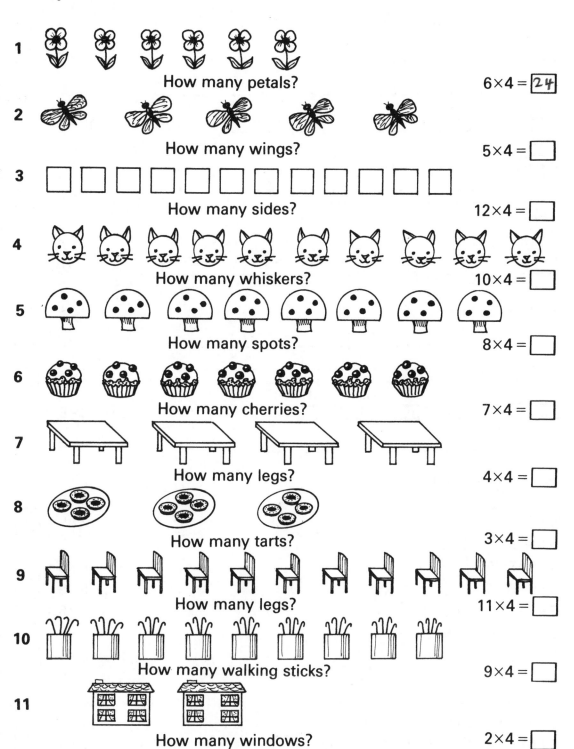

1 How many petals? $6 \times 4 = \boxed{24}$

2 How many wings? $5 \times 4 = \boxed{}$

3 How many sides? $12 \times 4 = \boxed{}$

4 How many whiskers? $10 \times 4 = \boxed{}$

5 How many spots? $8 \times 4 = \boxed{}$

6 How many cherries? $7 \times 4 = \boxed{}$

7 How many legs? $4 \times 4 = \boxed{}$

8 How many tarts? $3 \times 4 = \boxed{}$

9 How many legs? $11 \times 4 = \boxed{}$

10 How many walking sticks? $9 \times 4 = \boxed{}$

11 How many windows? $2 \times 4 = \boxed{}$

Groups of five

A Complete the equations.

$4 \times 5 = \square$

$6 \times 5 = \square$

$10 \times 5 = \square$

$3 \times 5 = \square$

$9 \times 5 = \square$

$1 \times 5 = \square$

$12 \times 5 = \square$

$2 \times 5 = \square$

$7 \times 5 = \square$

$11 \times 5 = \square$

$8 \times 5 = \square$

$5 \times 5 = \square$

B Copy and complete.

$0+5 = \boxed{5}$

$5+5 = \boxed{10}$

$5+5+5 = \square$

$5+5+5+5 = \square$

$5+5+5+5+5 = \square$

$5+5+5+5+5+5 = \square$

$5+5+5+5+5+5+5 = \square$

$5+5+5+5+5+5+5+5 = \square$

$5+5+5+5+5+5+5+5+5 = \square$

$5+5+5+5+5+5+5+5+5+5 = \square$

$5+5+5+5+5+5+5+5+5+5+5 = \square$

$5+5+5+5+5+5+5+5+5+5+5+5 = \square$

$1 \times 5 = \boxed{5}$

$2 \times 5 = \boxed{10}$

$3 \times 5 = \square$

$4 \times 5 = \square$

$5 \times 5 = \square$

$6 \times 5 = \square$

$7 \times 5 = \square$

$8 \times 5 = \square$

$9 \times 5 = \square$

$10 \times 5 = \square$

$11 \times 5 = \square$

$12 \times 5 = \square$

Groups of five

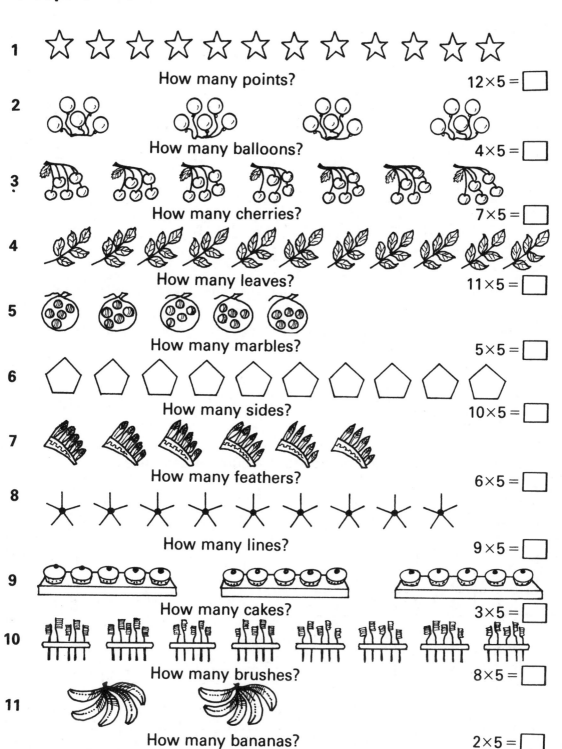

1 How many points? $12 \times 5 = \square$

2 How many balloons? $4 \times 5 = \square$

3 How many cherries? $7 \times 5 = \square$

4 How many leaves? $11 \times 5 = \square$

5 How many marbles? $5 \times 5 = \square$

6 How many sides? $10 \times 5 = \square$

7 How many feathers? $6 \times 5 = \square$

8 How many lines? $9 \times 5 = \square$

9 How many cakes? $3 \times 5 = \square$

10 How many brushes? $8 \times 5 = \square$

11 How many bananas? $2 \times 5 = \square$

Groups of six

A Complete the equations.

$10 \times 6 = \boxed{}$

$5 \times 6 = \boxed{}$

$12 \times 6 = \boxed{}$

$1 \times 6 = \boxed{}$

$3 \times 6 = \boxed{}$

$11 \times 6 = \boxed{}$

$2 \times 6 = \boxed{}$

$6 \times 6 = \boxed{}$

$8 \times 6 = \boxed{}$

$4 \times 6 = \boxed{}$

$9 \times 6 = \boxed{}$

$7 \times 6 = \boxed{}$

B Draw the stairway and complete the number sentences.

6											
6	6										
6	6	6									
6	6	6	6								
6	6	6	6	6							
6	6	6	6	6	6						
6	6	6	6	6	6	6					
6	6	6	6	6	6	6	6				
6	6	6	6	6	6	6	6	6			
6	6	6	6	6	6	6	6	6	6		
6	6	6	6	6	6	6	6	6	6	6	
6	6	6	6	6	6	6	6	6	6	6	6

$1 \times 6 = \boxed{}$

$2 \times 6 = \boxed{}$

$3 \times 6 = \boxed{}$

$4 \times 6 = \boxed{}$

$5 \times 6 = \boxed{}$

$6 \times 6 = \boxed{}$

$7 \times 6 = \boxed{}$

$8 \times 6 = \boxed{}$

$9 \times 6 = \boxed{}$

$10 \times 6 = \boxed{}$

$11 \times 6 = \boxed{}$

$12 \times 6 = \boxed{}$

Groups of six

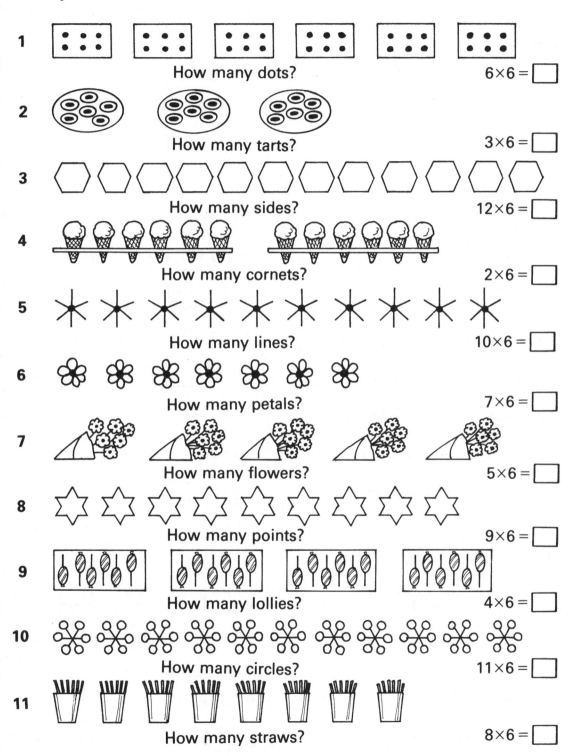

1 How many dots? $6 \times 6 = \boxed{}$

2 How many tarts? $3 \times 6 = \boxed{}$

3 How many sides? $12 \times 6 = \boxed{}$

4 How many cornets? $2 \times 6 = \boxed{}$

5 How many lines? $10 \times 6 = \boxed{}$

6 How many petals? $7 \times 6 = \boxed{}$

7 How many flowers? $5 \times 6 = \boxed{}$

8 How many points? $9 \times 6 = \boxed{}$

9 How many lollies? $4 \times 6 = \boxed{}$

10 How many circles? $11 \times 6 = \boxed{}$

11 How many straws? $8 \times 6 = \boxed{}$

Dividing by two

A Use counters to divide.

Put

1 12 counters into 2 groups $12 \div 2 = \square$

2 8 counters into 2 groups $8 \div 2 = \square$

3 24 counters into 2 groups $24 \div 2 = \square$

4 6 counters into 2 groups $6 \div 2 = \square$

5 20 counters into 2 groups $20 \div 2 = \square$

6 22 counters into 2 groups $22 \div 2 = \square$

7 4 counters into 2 groups $4 \div 2 = \square$

8 18 counters into 2 groups $18 \div 2 = \square$

9 16 counters into 2 groups $16 \div 2 = \square$

10 10 counters into 2 groups $10 \div 2 = \square$

11 2 counters into 2 groups $2 \div 2 = \square$

12 14 counters into 2 groups $14 \div 2 = \square$

B How many groups of 2 in

6? $6 \div 2 = \square$ 2? $2 \div 2 = \square$ 20? $20 \div 2 = \square$

16? $16 \div 2 = \square$ 14? $14 \div 2 = \square$ 12? $12 \div 2 = \square$

18? $18 \div 2 = \square$ 24? $24 \div 2 = \square$ 8? $8 \div 2 = \square$

10? $10 \div 2 = \square$ 4? $4 \div 2 = \square$ 22? $22 \div 2 = \square$

Dividing by three

A Use counters to divide.

Put

1 36 counters into 3 groups $36 \div 3 = \boxed{}$

2   9 counters into 3 groups $9 \div 3 = \boxed{}$

3 12 counters into 3 groups $12 \div 3 = \boxed{}$

4 24 counters into 3 groups $24 \div 3 = \boxed{}$

5 30 counters into 3 groups $30 \div 3 = \boxed{}$

6   3 counters into 3 groups $3 \div 3 = \boxed{}$

7 18 counters into 3 groups $18 \div 3 = \boxed{}$

8 27 counters into 3 groups $27 \div 3 = \boxed{}$

9 21 counters into 3 groups $21 \div 3 = \boxed{}$

10 33 counters into 3 groups $33 \div 3 = \boxed{}$

11   6 counters into 3 groups $6 \div 3 = \boxed{}$

12 15 counters into 3 groups $15 \div 3 = \boxed{}$

B How many groups of 3 in

36? $36 \div 3 = \boxed{}$ 9? $9 \div 3 = \boxed{}$ 3? $3 \div 3 = \boxed{}$

33? $33 \div 3 = \boxed{}$ 30? $30 \div 3 = \boxed{}$ 18? $18 \div 3 = \boxed{}$

15? $15 \div 3 = \boxed{}$ 27? $27 \div 3 = \boxed{}$ 24? $24 \div 3 = \boxed{}$

12? $12 \div 3 = \boxed{}$ 6? $6 \div 3 = \boxed{}$ 21? $21 \div 3 = \boxed{}$

Dividing by four

A Use counters to divide.
Put

1 36 counters into 4 groups $\qquad$ $36 \div 4 = \boxed{}$

2 16 counters into 4 groups $\qquad$ $16 \div 4 = \boxed{}$

3 8 counters into 4 groups $\qquad$ $8 \div 4 = \boxed{}$

4 48 counters into 4 groups $\qquad$ $48 \div 4 = \boxed{}$

5 24 counters into 4 groups $\qquad$ $24 \div 4 = \boxed{}$

6 32 counters into 4 groups $\qquad$ $32 \div 4 = \boxed{}$

7 20 counters into 4 groups $\qquad$ $20 \div 4 = \boxed{}$

8 28 counters into 4 groups $\qquad$ $28 \div 4 = \boxed{}$

9 40 counters into 4 groups $\qquad$ $40 \div 4 = \boxed{}$

10 44 counters into 4 groups $\qquad$ $44 \div 4 = \boxed{}$

11 12 counters into 4 groups $\qquad$ $12 \div 4 = \boxed{}$

12 4 counters into 4 groups $\qquad$ $4 \div 4 = \boxed{}$

B How many groups of 4 in

4? $\quad 4 \div 4 = \boxed{}$ $\qquad$ 20? $\quad 20 \div 4 = \boxed{}$ $\qquad$ 24? $\quad 24 \div 4 = \boxed{}$

12? $\quad 12 \div 4 = \boxed{}$ $\qquad$ 36? $\quad 36 \div 4 = \boxed{}$ $\qquad$ 40? $\quad 40 \div 4 = \boxed{}$

28? $\quad 28 \div 4 = \boxed{}$ $\qquad$ 16? $\quad 16 \div 4 = \boxed{}$ $\qquad$ 48? $\quad 48 \div 4 = \boxed{}$

44? $\quad 44 \div 4 = \boxed{}$ $\qquad$ 8? $\quad 8 \div 4 = \boxed{}$ $\qquad$ 32? $\quad 32 \div 4 = \boxed{}$

Dividing by five

A Use counters to divide.

Put

1 5 counters in groups of 5 $\qquad$ $5 \div 5 = \boxed{}$

2 35 counters in groups of 5 $\qquad$ $35 \div 5 = \boxed{}$

3 15 counters in groups of 5 $\qquad$ $15 \div 5 = \boxed{}$

4 60 counters in groups of 5 $\qquad$ $60 \div 5 = \boxed{}$

5 30 counters in groups of 5 $\qquad$ $30 \div 5 = \boxed{}$

6 55 counters in groups of 5 $\qquad$ $55 \div 5 = \boxed{}$

7 10 counters in groups of 5 $\qquad$ $10 \div 5 = \boxed{}$

8 40 counters in groups of 5 $\qquad$ $40 \div 5 = \boxed{}$

9 50 counters in groups of 5 $\qquad$ $50 \div 5 = \boxed{}$

10 25 counters in groups of 5 $\qquad$ $25 \div 5 = \boxed{}$

11 45 counters in groups of 5 $\qquad$ $45 \div 5 = \boxed{}$

12 20 counters in groups of 5 $\qquad$ $20 \div 5 = \boxed{}$

B How many groups of 5 in

60? $\quad 60 \div 5 = \boxed{}$ $\qquad$ 30? $\quad 30 \div 5 = \boxed{}$ $\qquad$ 10? $\quad 10 \div 5 = \boxed{}$

15? $\quad 15 \div 5 = \boxed{}$ $\qquad$ 35? $\quad 35 \div 5 = \boxed{}$ $\qquad$ 40? $\quad 40 \div 5 = \boxed{}$

5? $\quad 5 \div 5 = \boxed{}$ $\qquad$ 55? $\quad 55 \div 5 = \boxed{}$ $\qquad$ 50? $\quad 50 \div 5 = \boxed{}$

45? $\quad 45 \div 5 = \boxed{}$ $\qquad$ 20? $\quad 20 \div 5 = \boxed{}$ $\qquad$ 25? $\quad 25 \div 5 = \boxed{}$

Dividing by six

A   Use counters to divide.

Put

1   18 counters in groups of 6 $18 \div 6 = \boxed{}$

2   48 counters in groups of 6 $48 \div 6 = \boxed{}$

3   30 counters in groups of 6 $30 \div 6 = \boxed{}$

4   42 counters in groups of 6 $42 \div 6 = \boxed{}$

5   66 counters in groups of 6 $66 \div 6 = \boxed{}$

6   60 counters in groups of 6 $60 \div 6 = \boxed{}$

7   54 counters in groups of 6 $54 \div 6 = \boxed{}$

8   6 counters in groups of 6 $6 \div 6 = \boxed{}$

9   36 counters in groups of 6 $36 \div 6 = \boxed{}$

10   24 counters in groups of 6 $24 \div 6 = \boxed{}$

11   72 counters in groups of 6 $72 \div 6 = \boxed{}$

12   12 counters in groups of 6 $12 \div 6 = \boxed{}$

B   How many groups of 6 in

66? $66 \div 6 = \boxed{}$ 48? $48 \div 6 = \boxed{}$ 30? $30 \div 6 = \boxed{}$

12? $12 \div 6 = \boxed{}$ 6? $6 \div 6 = \boxed{}$ 72? $72 \div 6 = \boxed{}$

54? $54 \div 6 = \boxed{}$ 24? $24 \div 6 = \boxed{}$ 18? $18 \div 6 = \boxed{}$

60? $60 \div 6 = \boxed{}$ 42? $42 \div 6 = \boxed{}$ 36? $36 \div 6 = \boxed{}$

Division with remainders

A Use counters to divide.

19 counters put in groups of 4 = 4 remainder 3

1 Group each of these values in fours.

| 9 | 23 | 41 | 38 | 22 | 15 | 47 | 29 |

2 Group each of these values in twos.

| 23 | 20 | 17 | 13 | 7 | 16 | 19 | 21 |

3 Group each of these values in threes.

| 35 | 28 | 25 | 17 | 32 | 22 | 16 | 20 |

4 Group each of these values in fives.

| 59 | 34 | 18 | 58 | 21 | 44 | 39 | 9 |

5 Group each of these values in sixes.

| 28 | 63 | 45 | 32 | 58 | 17 | 51 | 71 |

B Copy and complete.

1
23 = ☐ twos rem ☐
23 = ☐ threes rem ☐
23 = ☐ fours rem ☐
23 = ☐ fives rem ☐
23 = ☐ sixes rem ☐

2
14 = ☐ twos rem ☐
14 = ☐ threes rem ☐
14 = ☐ fours rem ☐
14 = ☐ fives rem ☐
14 = ☐ sixes rem ☐

3
21 = ☐ twos rem ☐
21 = ☐ threes rem ☐
21 = ☐ fours rem ☐
21 = ☐ fives rem ☐
21 = ☐ sixes rem ☐

4
19 = ☐ twos rem ☐
19 = ☐ threes rem ☐
19 = ☐ fours rem ☐
19 = ☐ fives rem ☐
19 = ☐ sixes rem ☐

How much?

How much in each money bag?

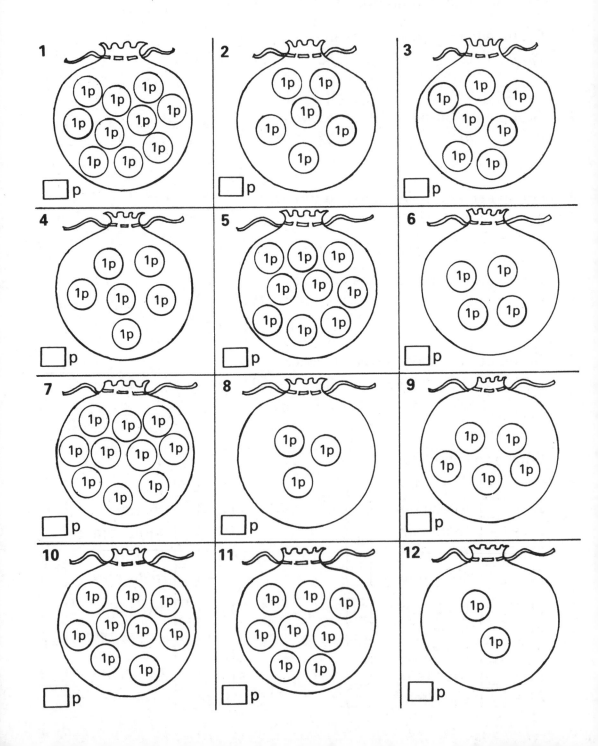

How much?

Count these amounts of money.

1 (2p) (2p) (2p) (2p) (2p) = ☐p

2 (2p) (2p) (2p) (2p) (1p) = ☐p

3 (2p) (2p) (2p) (2p) (1p)(1p) = ☐p

4 (2p) (2p) (2p)(1p)(1p)(1p)(1p) = ☐p

5 (2p) (1p) = ☐p

6 (2p) (2p) (1p)(1p)(1p)(1p) = ☐p

7 (2p) (2p) (2p) (1p) = ☐p

8 (2p) (2p) (1p) = ☐p

9 (2p) (1p)(1p)(1p)(1p)(1p)(1p) = ☐p

10 (2p) (1p) (1p) (1p) = ☐p

11 (2p) (2p) (2p) = ☐p

12 (2p) (2p) (1p) = ☐p

13 (2p) (1p)(1p)(1p) = ☐p

14 (2p) (1p)(1p)(1p)(1p)(1p)(1p)(1p) = ☐p

15 (2p) (2p) (2p) (1p)(1p)(1p) = ☐p

16 (2p) (2p) (1p)(1p)(1p)(1p)(1p)(1p) = ☐p

17 (2p) (1p)(1p)(1p)(1p)(1p)(1p)(1p)(1p) = ☐p

18 (2p) (2p) (1p)(1p)(1p)(1p)(1p) = ☐p

19 (2p) (2p) (1p)(1p)(1p) = ☐p

20 (2p) (1p)(1p)(1p)(1p)(1p) = ☐p

21 (2p) (1p) (1p) = ☐p

22 (2p) (2p) (2p) (1p)(1p) = ☐p

23 (2p) (2p) (2p) (2p) = ☐p

24 (2p) (2p) = ☐p

How much?

Count these amounts of money.

1. (5p) (2p) (1p) = ☐ p
2. (5p) (5p) (2p) (1p) = ☐ p

3. (5p) (5p) = ☐ p
4. (5p) (5p) (1p) = ☐ p

5. (5p) (5p) (5p) (2p) (1p) = ☐ p
6. (5p) (5p) (5p) (1p) = ☐ p

7. (5p) (5p) (5p) (1p) (1p) (1p) = ☐ p
8. (5p) (5p) (5p) (2p) = ☐ p

9. (5p) (2p) = ☐ p
10. (5p) (5p) (2p) (1p) (1p) (1p) = ☐ p

11. (5p) (5p) (5p) = ☐ p
12. (5p) (5p) (5p) (2p) (2p) (1p) = ☐ p

13. (5p) (5p) (5p) (2p) (2p) = ☐ p
14. (5p) (5p) (2p) (1p) (1p) = ☐ p

15. (5p) (5p) (5p) (5p) = ☐ p
16. (5p) (5p) (1p) (1p) (1p) = ☐ p

17. (5p) (5p) (2p) (2p) = ☐ p
18. (5p) (2p) (1p) (1p) = ☐ p

19. (5p) (5p) (5p) (2p) (1p) (1p) = ☐ p
20. (5p) (1p) (1p) = ☐ p

21. (5p) (5p) (2p) = ☐ p
22. (5p) (1p) = ☐ p

23. (5p) (2p) (2p) = ☐ p
24. (5p) (5p) (2p) (2p) (1p) = ☐ p

Using 1p, 2p and 5p coins

2p

5p

1p

A Find 3 different ways of paying for each of these things using only 1p, 2p and 5p coins.

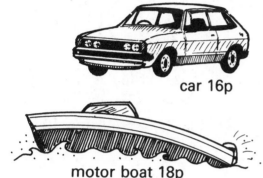
car 16p

motor boat 18p

doll 19p

book 20p

B Which 2 coins make the following amounts?
  1 4p   **2** 7p   **3** 6p   **4** 3p   **5** 10p

C Which 3 coins make the following amounts?
  1 9p   **2** 8p   **3** 5p   **4** 11p   **5** 15p

D Which 4 coins make the following amounts?
  1 20p   **2** 16p   **3** 7p   **4** 13p   **5** 14p

  6 10p   **7** 17p   **8** 8p   **9** 12p   **10** 9p

E Which 5 coins make the following amounts?
1 17p   **2** 19p   **3** 14p   **4** 10p   **5** 18p

Making 10p

10p

A Each line of coins should make 10p — which coin is missing?

1 (2p) (2p) (2p) (2p) [?]   **2** (2p) (2p) (2p) (2p) (1p) [?]

3 (5p) (2p) (2p) [?]   **4** (2p) (2p) (1p) [?]

5 (2p) (2p) (2p) (1p) (1p) [?]   **6** (2p) (5p) (1p) [?]

7 (5p) [?]   **8** (5p) (1p) (1p) (1p) [?]

9 (1p) (1p) (1p) (5p) (1p) [?]   **10** (1p) (1p) (1p) (1p) (1p) [?]

B These money bags should each hold 10p — which coins are missing?

1 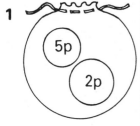 **2** 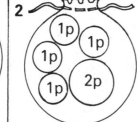 **3** 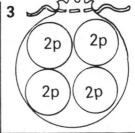 **4**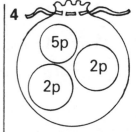

5 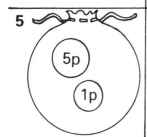 **6** 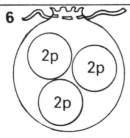 **7** 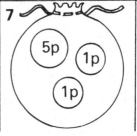 **8**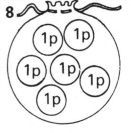

Shopping with 10p

liquorice 2p	chocolate mouse 3p	sherbet 4p	dummy 5p	laces 2p
toffee lolly 3p	bubble gum 1p	chewing gum 3p	pear drop 1p	teddy bear 2p

Get your own coins to find the cost of these.

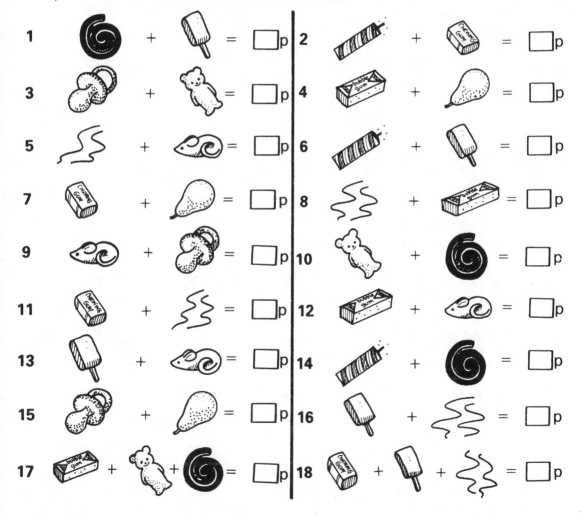

1 + = ☐p   2 + = ☐p

3 + = ☐p   4 + = ☐p

5 + = ☐p   6 + = ☐p

7 + = ☐p   8 + = ☐p

9 + = ☐p   10 + = ☐p

11 + = ☐p   12 + = ☐p

13 + = ☐p   14 + = ☐p

15 + = ☐p   16 + = ☐p

17 + + = ☐p   18 + + = ☐p

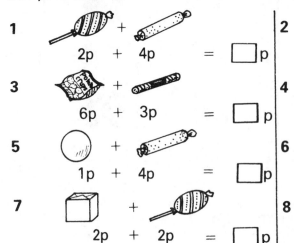
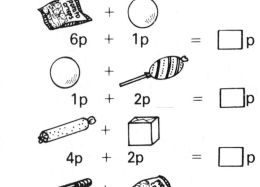
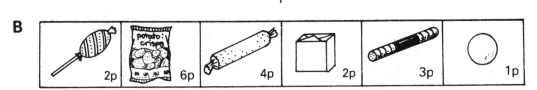

Addition to 10p

A Add these amount of money.

1 (5p)(1p) + (2p)(1p)

6p + 3p   = ☐ p

2 (2p)(2p) + (2p)(1p)

4p + 3p   = ☐ p

3 (5p)(2p) + (2p)(1p)

7p + 3p   = ☐ p

4 (2p)(2p)(2p) + (2p)(1p)

6p + 3p   = ☐ p

5 (2p)(1p) + (2p)(2p)(1p)

3p + 5p   = ☐ p

6 (2p)(2p)(1p) + (2p)

5p + 2p   = ☐ p

7 (5p)(2p) + (1p)(1p)

7p + 2p   = ☐ p

8 (2p)(2p)(2p) + (1p)(1p)

6p + 2p   = ☐ p

B

2p	6p	4p	2p	3p	1p

Get your own coins to find the cost of these.

1 +

2p + 4p   = ☐ p

2 +

6p + 1p   = ☐ p

3 +

6p + 3p   = ☐ p

4 +

1p + 2p   = ☐ p

5 +

1p + 4p   = ☐ p

6 +

4p + 2p   = ☐ p

7 +

2p + 2p   = ☐ p

8 +

3p + 6p   = ☐ p

Change from 5p

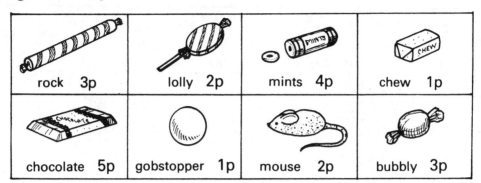

| rock 3p | lolly 2p | mints 4p | chew 1p |
| chocolate 5p | gobstopper 1p | mouse 2p | bubbly 3p |

Use coins to help you.
How much change if I buy

1 a stick of rock?   3p + ☐p = 5p

2 mints?   4p + ☐p = 5p

3 chocolate?   5p + ☐p = 5p

4 a lolly?   2p + ☐p = 5p

5 a chew?   1p + ☐p = 5p

6 a bubbly?   3p + ☐p = 5p

7 a mouse?   2p + ☐p = 5p

8 a gobstopper?   1p + ☐p = 5p

9 a gobstopper and a mouse?   1p + 2p + ☐p = 5p

10 a lolly and a chew?   2p + 1p + ☐p = 5p

11 a bubbly and a lolly?   3p + 2p + ☐p = 5p

12 mints and a gobstopper? 4p + 1p + ☐p = 5p

Change from 10p

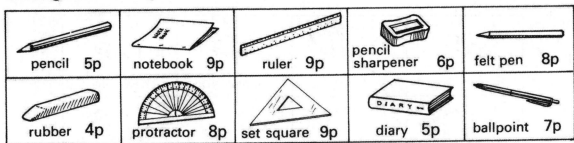

| pencil 5p | notebook 9p | ruler 9p | pencil sharpener 6p | felt pen 8p |
| rubber 4p | protractor 8p | set square 9p | diary 5p | ballpoint 7p |

Use coins to help you.

A How much change if I buy.

1 a notebook? $9p + \boxed{}p = 10p$

2 a ballpoint? $7p + \boxed{}p = 10p$

3 a protractor? $8p + \boxed{}p = 10p$

4 a ruler? $9p + \boxed{}p = 10p$

5 a pencil? $5p + \boxed{}p = 10p$

6 a pencil sharpener? $6p + \boxed{}p = 10p$

7 a felt pen? $8p + \boxed{}p = 10p$

8 a set square? $9p + \boxed{}p = 10p$

9 a diary? $5p + \boxed{}p = 10p$

10 a rubber? $4p + \boxed{}p = 10p$

11 a pencil and a rubber? $5p + 4p + \boxed{}p = 10p$

12 a diary and a rubber? $5p + 4p + \boxed{}p = 10p$

B Say which coins you receive in change each time.

How much?

How much money on each line?

1 (10p)(2p)(2p)(5p)(1p) = ☐ p

2 (2p)(1p)(1p)(1p)(5p)(10p) = ☐ p

3 (2p)(2p)(2p)(2p)(1p)(10p) = ☐ p

4 (5p)(5p)(5p)(2p)(2p) = ☐ p

5 (10p)(2p)(2p)(1p)(1p) = ☐ p

6 (5p)(1p)(1p)(10p) = ☐ p

7 (10p)(2p)(2p)(1p) = ☐ p

8 (5p)(10p)(1p)(1p)(1p) = ☐ p

9 (10p)(2p)(2p)(2p)(1p) = ☐ p

10 (5p)(2p)(2p)(2p)(2p) = ☐ p

11 (2p)(10p)(5p)(1p) = ☐ p

12 (10p)(2p)(1p)(1p)(1p) = ☐ p

Using 10p, 5p, 2p and 1p coins

A Use coins to make up these amounts of money using the least number of coins.

1 7p	**2** 3p	**3** 19p	**4** 13p
5 10p	**6** 15p	**7** 9p	**8** 16p
9 12p	**10** 18p	**11** 11p	**12** 8p
13 6p	**14** 14p	**15** 17p	**16** 4p

B Use coins to help you.

Write 3 coins which make these amounts.
   1 11p   **2** 16p   **3** 12p   **4** 15p   **5** 17p   **6** 13p

Write 4 coins which make these amounts.
   1 16p   **2** 15p   **3** 19p   **4** 14p   **5** 12p   **6** 18p

Write 5 coins which make these amounts.
   1 19p   **2** 18p   **3** 15p   **4** 17p   **5** 14p   **6** 16p

C Make up each amount in 3 ways.

1 12p	**2** 7p	**3** 14p	**4** 11p	**5** 18p	**6** 9p
7 15p	**8** 10p	**9** 13p	**10** 17p	**11** 8p	**12** 16p

Values up to 20p

Each line should make 20p.
Which coin is missing?

1. (20p) = (5p)(5p)(2p)(2p)(1p) = ☐ p

2. (20p) = (10p)(5p)(2p)(1p) = ☐ p

3. (20p) = (5p)(2p)(2p)(2p)(2p)(5p) = ☐ p

4. (20p) = (2p)(10p)(2p)(1p) = ☐ p

5. (20p) = (5p)(2p)(2p)(2p)(1p)(2p)(5p) = ☐ p

6. (20p) = (2p)(1p)(2p)(2p)(2p)(1p) = ☐ p

7. (20p) = (5p)(5p)(5p) = ☐ p

8. (20p) = (1p)(2p)(1p)(2p)(2p)(10p) = ☐ p

9. (20p) = (5p)(2p)(2p)(2p)(2p)(2p) = ☐ p

10. (20p) = (1p)(10p)(1p)(2p)(5p) = ☐ p

11. (20p) = (10p)(5p)(1p)(1p)(1p)(1p) = ☐ p

12. (20p) = (2p)(2p)(2p)(2p)(10p) = ☐ p

Values up to 20p

Each line should make 20p.

A   Use your coins to find the missing amount.

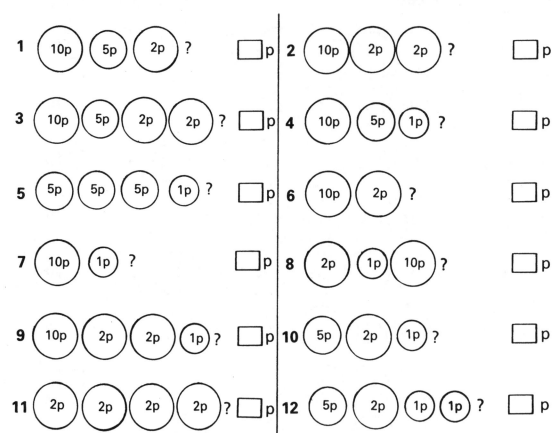

1 (10p) (5p) (2p) ?   ☐p   **2** (10p) (2p) (2p) ?   ☐p

3 (10p) (5p) (2p) (2p) ?   ☐p   **4** (10p) (5p) (1p) ?   ☐p

5 (5p) (5p) (5p) (1p) ?   ☐p   **6** (10p) (2p) ?   ☐p

7 (10p) (1p) ?   ☐p   **8** (2p) (1p) (10p) ?   ☐p

9 (10p) (2p) (2p) (1p) ?   ☐p   **10** (5p) (2p) (1p) ?   ☐p

11 (2p) (2p) (2p) (2p) ?   ☐p   **12** (5p) (2p) (1p) (1p) ?   ☐p

B   Use coins to help you.

How much must be added to these amounts to make 20p?

1 15p   **2** 12p   **3** 16p   **4** 17p   **5** 13p   **6** 4p   **7** 11p

8 19p   **9** 14p   **10** 10p   **11** 7p   **12** 9p   **13** 18p   **14** 6p

Shopping with 15p

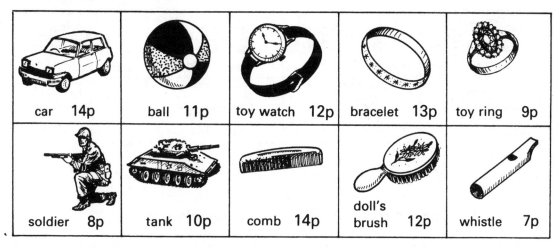

| car 14p | ball 11p | toy watch 12p | bracelet 13p | toy ring 9p |
| soldier 8p | tank 10p | comb 14p | doll's brush 12p | whistle 7p |

A Copy and complete this table.
Use coins to help you.

bought	cost	change from 15p	coins given in change
soldier			
ball			
comb			
whistle			
doll's brush			
toy watch			
bracelet			
tank			
car			
toy ring			

B Draw the coins you would give if you gave the exact money for these.

1 tank
2 toy ring
3 bracelet
4 toy watch
5 doll's brush
6 ball
7 comb
8 whistle
9 soldier
10 car

Shopping with 20p

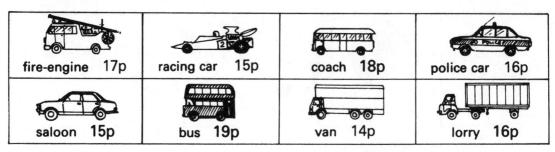

fire-engine 17p	racing car 15p	coach 18p	police car 16p
saloon 15p	bus 19p	van 14p	lorry 16p

A Copy and complete the table. Use coins to help you.

bought	cost	change from 20p	coins given in change
van			
fire-engine			
police car			
lorry			
bus			
coach			
saloon			
racing car			

B Copy and complete.

bought	coins used if the exact money was given
racing car	
police car	
van	
coach	
bus	
saloon	
lorry	
fire-engine	

Shopping with 15p

| lion 7p | hyena 3p | camel 5p | giraffe 7p | elephant 7p |
| tiger 5p | zebra 6p | kangaroo 6p | monkey 4p | antelope 6p |

A Copy and complete this table.
Use coins to help you.

bought	cost	change from 15p
lion+tiger	7p + 5p = ☐ p	☐ p
camel+zebra		
giraffe+monkey		
elephant+antelope		
hyena+kangaroo		
elephant+tiger		
camel+kangaroo		
antelope+lion		
giraffe+zebra		
monkey+hyena		
lion+monkey		
tiger+antelope		
zebra+hyena		
elephant+kangaroo		
giraffe+camel		

B Write which coins you would receive in change if you bought
1 a lion and a giraffe
2 a zebra and an antelope
3 a camel and a monkey
4 a hyena and an elephant
5 a tiger and a kangaroo

Shopping with 20p

parrot 8p	thrush 6p	duck 6p	kingfisher 7p	ostrich 9p
eagle 9p	sparrow 5p	owl 7p	emu 9p	hawk 8p

Copy and complete the table.
Use coins to help you.

bought	cost	change from 20p
parrot+owl	8p +7p = ☐ p	
hawk+eagle		
sparrow+duck		
kingfisher+emu		
ostrich+thrush		
kingfisher+owl		
parrot+duck		
thrush+hawk		
eagle+emu		
ostrich+sparrow		
emu+duck		
hawk+owl		
eagle+parrot		
thrush+sparrow		
kingfisher+ostrich		
duck+eagle		
hawk+parrot		
thrush+emu		
ostrich+owl		
sparrow+kingfisher		

The cake shop

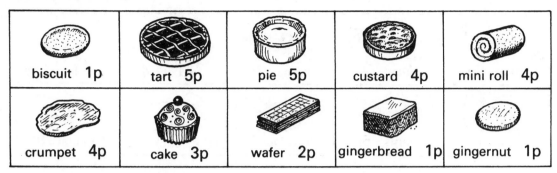

| biscuit 1p | tart 5p | pie 5p | custard 4p | mini roll 4p |
| crumpet 4p | cake 3p | wafer 2p | gingerbread 1p | gingernut 1p |

A Copy and complete.
Use coins to help you.

bought	cost of one	total cost	change from 15p
2 tarts	5p	2 (5p) = 10p	5p
3 custards			
2 mini rolls			
2 wafers			
2 crumpets			
3 cakes			
2 gingernuts			
4 biscuits			
5 gingerbreads			
3 pies			
3 mini rolls			
2 pies			
4 wafers			
7 biscuits			
9 gingernuts			
5 cakes			
2 custards			
3 crumpets			

B How many of each of these could you buy with 15p?

| **1** biscuits | **2** tarts | **3** pies |
| **4** cakes | **5** gingerbreads | **6** gingernuts |

The sweet shop

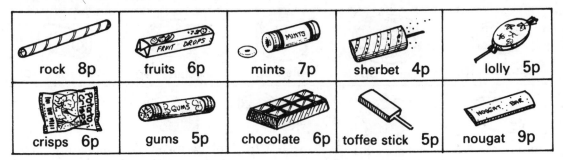

| rock 8p | fruits 6p | mints 7p | sherbet 4p | lolly 5p |
| crisps 6p | gums 5p | chocolate 6p | toffee stick 5p | nougat 9p |

A Copy and complete.
Use coins to help you.

bought	cost of one	total cost	change from 20p
2 sticks of rock	8p	2 (8p) = 16p	4p
3 tubes of fruits			
2 nougats			
2 tubes of gums			
3 bags of crisps			
3 lollies			
2 sherbets			
2 tubes of mints			
2 bars of chocolate			
3 toffee sticks			
2 tubes of fruits			
2 toffee sticks			
3 bars of chocolate			
4 tubes of gums			
2 lollies			
4 sherbets			
2 bags of crisps			
3 sherbets			
3 tubes of gums			
4 toffee sticks			
5 sherbets			
4 lollies			

Time — o'clock

A Write the times shown on these clocks.

3 o'clock	7 o'clock	4 o'clock	12 o'clock
1 o'clock	8 o'clock	10 o'clock	6 o'clock
5 o'clock	9 o'clock	11 o'clock	2 o'clock

B Draw clocks to show these times.

ten o'clock	eleven o'clock	two o'clock	eight o'clock
three o'clock	four o'clock	seven o'clock	one o'clock
twelve o'clock	nine o'clock	five o'clock	six o'clock

Time — half past

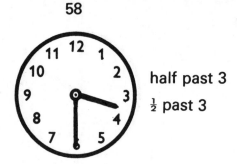

half past 3

½ past 3

A Write the times shown on these clocks.

PAST

TO

half past 6   half past 1   half past 8   half past 9

half past 2   half past 7   half past 12   half past 4

half past 5   half past 11   half past 3   half past 10

B Draw clocks to show these times.

½ past twelve   ½ past four   ½ past seven   ½ past one
½ past three   ½ past nine   ½ past two   ½ past ten
½ past eight   ½ past six   ½ past eleven   ½ past five

Time — quarter past

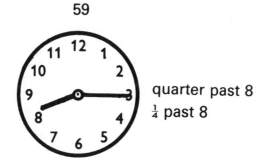

quarter past 8
$\frac{1}{4}$ past 8

A Write the times shown on these clocks.

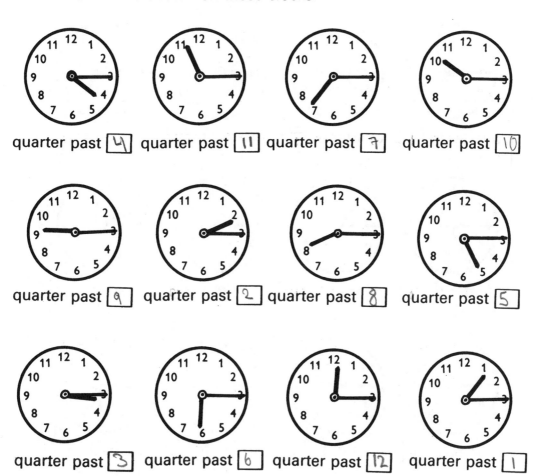

quarter past 4 quarter past 11 quarter past 7 quarter past 10

quarter past 9 quarter past 2 quarter past 8 quarter past 5

quarter past 3 quarter past 6 quarter past 12 quarter past 1

B Draw clocks to show these times.

$\frac{1}{4}$ past five $\frac{1}{4}$ past eight $\frac{1}{4}$ past seven $\frac{1}{4}$ past one
$\frac{1}{4}$ past nine $\frac{1}{4}$ past two $\frac{1}{4}$ past twelve $\frac{1}{4}$ past six
$\frac{1}{4}$ past three $\frac{1}{4}$ past eleven $\frac{1}{4}$ past four $\frac{1}{4}$ past ten

Time — quarter to

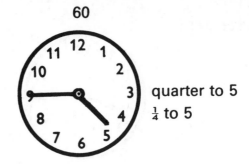

quarter to 5
$\frac{1}{4}$ to 5

A Write the times shown on these clocks.

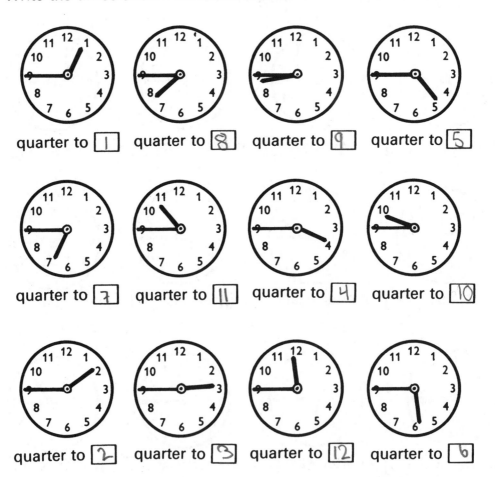

quarter to ☐ 1

quarter to ☐ 8

quarter to ☐ 9

quarter to ☐ 5

quarter to ☐ 7

quarter to ☐ 11

quarter to ☐ 4

quarter to ☐ 10

quarter to ☐ 2

quarter to ☐ 3

quarter to ☐ 12

quarter to ☐ 6

B Draw clocks to show these times.

$\frac{1}{4}$ to seven	$\frac{1}{4}$ to six	$\frac{1}{4}$ to eight	$\frac{1}{4}$ to two
$\frac{1}{4}$ to three	$\frac{1}{4}$ to one	$\frac{1}{4}$ to twelve	$\frac{1}{4}$ to ten
$\frac{1}{4}$ to eleven	$\frac{1}{4}$ to five	$\frac{1}{4}$ to nine	$\frac{1}{4}$ to four

The calendar

DECEMBER						
Sunday	Monday	Tuesday	Wednesday	Thursday	Friday	Saturday
	1	2	3	4	5	6
7	8	9	10	11	12	13
14	15	16	17	18	19	20
21	22	23	24	25	26	27
28	29	30	31			

1 Write down the day of the week on which each of these dates fall.

1st	18th	25th	12th	31st
29th	6th	23rd	15th	10th

2 On what day is the first day of the month?
3 On what day is the last day of the month?
4 How many Saturdays in December?
5 Are there more Saturdays or Wednesdays in this month?
6 How many Mondays are in this month?
7 Give the dates of the Thursdays.
8 Now give the dates of the Tuesdays.
9 How many days from Monday 1st to the next Monday?
10 How many days make a week?

Length

A

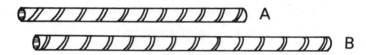

1 Which is the longer straw?

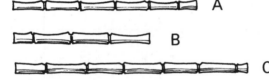

2 Which is the shorter crayon?

3

Which is the longest screw?
Which is the shortest screw?

4

Which is the shortest cane?
Which is the longest cane?

B Find the length of each object.

1
 ☐ cm

2 ☐ cm

3
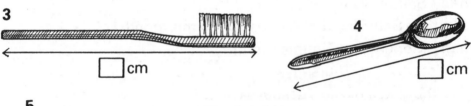 ☐ cm

4  ☐ cm

5
 ☐ cm

Mass

1 kg or 1000 g   ½ kg or 500 g   ¼ kg or 250 g

A Write the weight which makes each scale balance.

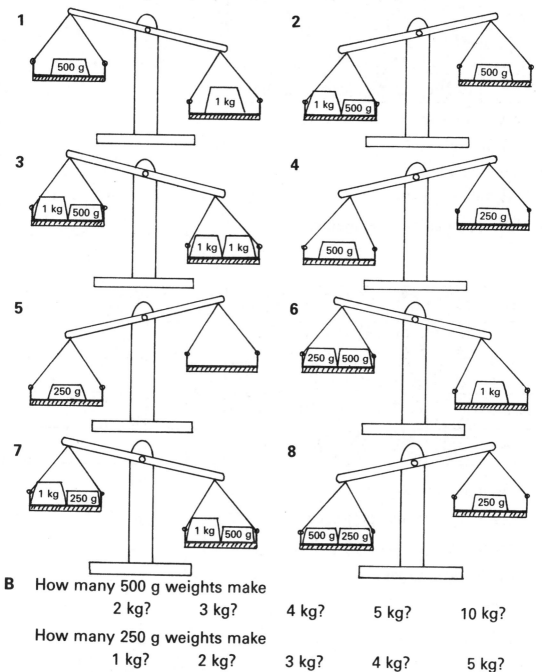

B How many 500 g weights make

　　　2 kg?　　　3 kg?　　　4 kg?　　　5 kg?　　　10 kg?

　　How many 250 g weights make

　　　1 kg?　　　2 kg?　　　3 kg?　　　4 kg?　　　5 kg?

Graphs — pictograms

A

horses									
pigs									
sheep									
cows									

1 How many cows?

2 How many sheep?

3 How many horses?

4 How many pigs?

5 How many animals altogether?

B

apples										
pears										
cherries										
oranges										
grapes										

1 How many pears?

2 How many bunches of grapes?

3 How many bunches of cherries?

4 How many oranges?

5 How many apples?

Answers

Page 2 Groups
1 elephants 2   **2** fish 6   **3** mice 7   **4** hats 7   **5** boats 5   **6** apples 6
7 cats 8   **8** wigwams 3   **9** lollipops 10   **10** cars 4   **11** flowerpots 8
12 skittles 9   **13** bows 10   **14** straws 9   **15** caravans 5

Page 3 Addition
1 9   **2** 6   **3** 7   **4** 3   **5** 8   **6** 9   **7** 4   **8** 10   **9** 9   **10** 6   **11** 5   **12** 9   **13** 8
14 8   **15** 7

Page 4 Addition
1 2   **2** 10   **3** 5   **4** 9   **5** 10   **6** 3   **7** 10   **8** 8   **9** 10   **10** 7   **11** 6   **12** 8

Page 5 Addition
1 $6 + 2 = 8$ **2** $5 + 5 = 10$ **3** $6 + 4 = 10$;   **4** $7 + 2 = 9$ **5** $5 + 4 = 9$ **6** $8 + 2 = 10$;
7 $3 + 3 = 6$ **8** $3 + 7 = 10$ **9** $4 + 4 = 8$;   **10** $2 + 5 = 7$ **11** $3 + 4 = 7$ **12** $7 + 3 = 10$

Page 6 Number families
A $5 + 0 = 5$ $4 + 1 = 5$ $3 + 2 = 5$ $2 + 3 = 5$ $1 + 4 = 5$ $0 + 5 = 5$
B $6 + 0 = 6$ $5 + 1 = 6$ $4 + 2 = 6$ $3 + 3 = 6$ $2 + 4 = 6$ $1 + 5 = 6$ $0 + 6 = 6$
C $7 + 0 = 7$ $6 + 1 = 7$ $5 + 2 = 7$ $4 + 3 = 7$ $3 + 4 = 7$ $2 + 5 = 7$ $1 + 6 = 7$
$0 + 7 = 7$
D $8 + 0 = 8$ $7 + 1 = 8$ $6 + 2 = 8$ $5 + 3 = 8$ $4 + 4 = 8$ $3 + 5 = 8$ $2 + 6 = 8$
$1 + 7 = 8$ $0 + 8 = 8$

Page 7 More number families
A $9 + 0 = 9$ $8 + 1 = 9$ $7 + 2 = 9$ $6 + 3 = 9$ $5 + 4 = 9$ $4 + 5 = 9$ $3 + 6 = 9$
$2 + 7 = 9$ $1 + 8 = 9$ $0 + 9 = 9$
$10 + 0 = 10$ $9 + 1 = 10$ $8 + 2 = 10$ $7 + 3 = 10$ $6 + 4 = 10$ $5 + 5 = 10$
$4 + 6 = 10$ $3 + 7 = 10$ $2 + 8 = 10$ $1 + 9 = 10$ $0 + 10 = 10$
B 1 4   **2** 4   **3** 5;   **4** 6   **5** 4   **6** 3;   **7** 3   **8** 7   **9** 3;   **10** 2   **11** 2   **12** 3;
13 5   **14** 4   **15** 6

Page 8 Subtraction
1 3   **2** 3   **3** 4;   **4** 3   **5** 1   **6** 2;   **7** 0   **8** 5   **9** 4;   **10** 4   **11** 5   **12** 6;
13 7   **14** 6   **15** 5

Page 9 Subtraction
1 $9 - 4 = 5$ **2** $10 - 3 = 7$ **3** $7 - 2 = 5$;   **4** $8 - 6 = 2$ **5** $4 - 3 = 1$ **6** $6 - 6 = 0$;
7 $5 - 4 = 1$ **8** $3 - 1 = 2$ **9** $2 - 1 = 1$;   **10** $10 - 6 = 4$ **11** $9 - 5 = 4$ **12** $7 - 4 = 3$

Page 10 Subtraction
1 $7 - 3 = 4$ **2** $10 - 5 = 5$ **3** $9 - 3 = 6$;   **4** $8 - 3 = 5$ **5** $4 - 2 = 2$ **6** $3 - 2 = 1$;
7 $8 - 2 = 6$ **8** $2 - 1 = 1$ **9** $9 - 2 = 7$;   **10** $9 - 8 = 1$ **11** $5 - 3 = 2$ **12** $7 - 1 = 6$

Page 11 Addition — number lines
A 5, 9, 3, 10;   6, 8, 7, 4
B 6, 8, 10, 9;   7
C 4, 7, 9, 6;   3, 5, 8, 10
D 6, 9, 5, 10;   7, 4, 8
E 10, 5, 8, 7;   9, 6

Page 12 Subtraction — number lines
A 6, 0, 3, 1, 5;   2, 4
B 2, 5, 8, 1, 3;   7, 0, 4, 6
C 4, 1, 3, 0, 2
D 0, 2, 4, 1, 3; 5
E 2, 1, 3, 6, 0;   7, 5, 4
F 4, 6, 1, 7, 3;   9, 5, 0, 8, 2

Page 13 More and less than
A 9, 1, 8;   10, 5, 1;   9, 3, 5;   10, 3, 1;   8, 2, 4;   9, 5, 8;   9, 2, 4;   9, 4, 0;
10, 0, 7
B 8 > 1, 4 < 8, 5 > 4;   1 < 6, 1 = 1, 6 < 8;   3 < 5, 4 > 2, 3 < 6;
4 < 5, 3 < 9, 2 < 6;   2 < 9, 2 < 3, 1 < 3;   10 > 2, 9 > 7, 7 > 1;
3 < 9, 1 < 10, 9 > 7;   5 < 9, 8 > 5, 7 > 2;   9 > 8, 5 > 2, 3 < 7;
7 > 4, 6 < 10, 10 > 5;   6 > 4, 10 > 6, 2 > 1;   5 < 10, 8 > 3, 4 < 8
C Check your child's answers are correct.

Page 14 Using the equaliser
A 6 + **3** = 9   3 + 2 = **5**   5 + **5** = 10   5 + **2** = 7;
2 + 4 = 6   4 + **4** = 8   7 + 2 = **9**   **7** + 2 = 9;
5 + 3 = **8**   **8** + 1 = 9   **2** + 6 = 8   3 + **0** = 3;
2 + **2** = 4   8 + 2 = **10**   3 + **7** = 10   3 + 4 = **7**;
1 + 6 = 7   4 + 4 = **8**   3 + 3 = **6**   **0** + 8 = 8;
6 + 4 = **10**   1 + **4** = 5   2 + **4** = 6   8 + **2** = 10
B 6 + 3 = 4 + **5**,   **3** + 1 = 2 + 2;   2 + 5 = **3** + 4,   5 + 5 = **6** + 4;
3 + 7 = 8 + **2**,   1 + **8** = 7 + 2;   4 + 4 = 5 + **3**,   5 + 2 = **4** + 3;
2 + 3 = 1 + 4,   **8** + 2 = 1 + 9;   **5** + 1 = 3 + 3,   2 + 4 = 4 + **2**
C 4 + 2 + 2 = 5 + **3**,   1 + **3** + 1 = 3 + 2;   3 + 4 = 2 + 3 + **2**,   6 + 3 = 2 + 4 + **3**;
6 + 2 + 1 = 3 + 2 + 1 + **3**,   **4** + 2 = 1 + 1 + 4;   **5** + 2 + 1 = 6 + 2,   8 + 2 = 4 + **4** + 2;
4 + **4** + 2 = 7 + 3,   3 + 1 = 1 + 2 + 1;   2 + 2 + 2 = 1 + **5**,   3 + 2 + 3 = 2 + **6**;
3 + 3 + **3** = 4 + 5,   7 + 2 + 1 = 5 + **5**;   6 + 0 = 3 + 1 + **2**,   **5** + 4 = 2 + 3 + 4;
1 + 4 = 2 + 1 + **2**,   2 + 5 = 3 + 3 + **1**;   6 + 1 + **0** = 3 + 4,   6 + 1 + **3** = 2 + 5 + 3

Page 15 Addition — number ladder
A 13, 20, 11, 15;   19, 14, 17, 16;   18, 12, 10
B 15, 20, 18, 14;   19, 16, 17, 13
C 19, 15, 17, 20;   13, 18, 14, 16
D 20, 15, 18, 17;   19, 13, 16, 14
E 20, 18, 19, 16;   17, 15, 13, 12

F 20, 13, 17, 19;   14, 12, 16, 18;   17, 11
G 16, 19, 11, 20;   13, 18, 15, 12;   14, 10, 17
H 20, 14, 18, 16;   15, 17, 12, 11;   19, 13
I 20, 9, 18, 11;   19, 16, 12, 15;   13, 17, 10

Page 16 Subtraction — number ladder
A 7, 14, 8, 15;   5, 9, 11, 13;   6, 10, 12
B 1, 9, 7, 3;   10, 11, 5, 6;   4, 8, 2
C 5, 12, 14, 7;   6, 13, 10, 8;   11, 4, 9
D 6, 13, 3, 11;   8, 9, 5, 10;   12, 7, 4
E 6, 13, 8, 14;   15, 10, 7, 12;   9, 16, 11
F 5, 9, 4, 2;   12, 10, 8, 6;   3, 11, 7
G 2, 5, 0, 10;   7, 3, 6, 9;   1, 8, 4
H 17, 7, 10, 14;   16, 9, 13, 15;   11, 8, 12

Page 17 Addition and subtraction — mapping
1 11, 15, 17, 20, 13, 12   **2** 9, 17, 8, 7, 12, 10   **3** 20, 18, 17, 19, 14, 15
4 15, 20, 13, 12, 11, 14   **5** 20, 7, 3, 2, 6, 5   **6** 9, 6, 8, 7, 4, 14

Page 18 The hundred square — tens
A 35, 44, 57, 32, 61, 70, 95, 47;   66, 88, 49, 38, 43, 69, 26, 52
B 31, 53, 19, 44, 78, 7, 42, 14;   26, 59, 65, 10, 4, 86, 71, 62
C 1 13, 23, 33, **43, 53, 63, 73, 83**, 93   **2** 45, **55, 65, 75, 85**, 95
3 7, 17, 27, 37, 47, 57, **67, 77, 87, 97**   **4** 12, **22, 32, 42**, 52, **62, 72, 82**, 92
5 8, **18**, 28, **38, 48, 58**, 68, **78, 88**, 98   **6** 36, 46, **56, 66, 76, 86**, 96
7 24, **34, 44, 54, 64, 74, 84**, 94   **8** 9, **19, 29, 39, 49, 59**, 69, **79, 89**, 99

Page 19 The abacus — tens and ones
A 2 6,   4 5,   1 4,   7 1,   5 8,   4 0;   5 2,   3 7,   9 7,   6 3,   8 3,   0 9
B Check your child's abaci reflect the numbers shown.
C 2, 7, 6, 4, 8, 3, 1, 5, 9

Page 20 More tens and ones
A 42, 51, 35, 67
B

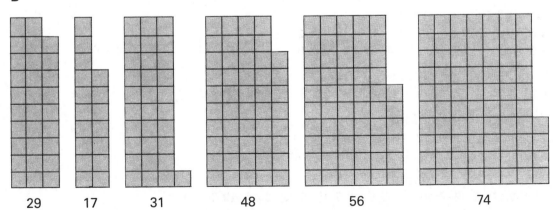

29   17   31   48   56   74

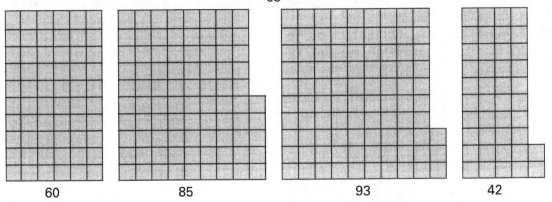

60   85   93   42

C 11 → 1 ten and 1 one, 67 → 6 tens and 7 ones, 33 → 3 tens and 3 ones,
26 → 2 tens and 6 ones, 42 → 4 tens and 2 ones, 38 → 3 tens and 8 ones,
55 → 5 tens and 5 ones, 64 → 6 tens and 4 ones;
79 → 7 tens and 9 ones, 68 → 6 tens and 8 ones, 92 → 9 tens and 2 ones,
60 → 6 tens and 0 ones, 54 → 5 tens and 4 ones, 23 → 2 tens and 3 ones,
15 → 1 ten and 5 ones, 36 → 3 tens and 6 ones;
87 → 8 tens and 7 ones, 72 → 7 tens and 2 ones, 50 → 5 tens and 0 ones,
41 → 4 tens and 1 one

Page 21 Addition and subtraction — tens and ones
A 47, 67, 89, 88; 39, 26, 69, 88; 29, 79, 99, 89; 59, 99, 77, 98; 18, 89, 98, 99
B 23, 44, 13, 22; 31, 62, 16, 13; 23, 32, 13, 21; 42, 22, 11, 12; 32, 32, 21, 23;
53, 21, 10, 14; 34, 15, 62, 1
C 9, 5, 7, 6, 1, 8; 4, 2, 3, 10

Page 22 Groups of two
A 2, 24, 14, 10, 22, 18; 12, 8, 20, 16, 4, 6
B 2, 4, 6, 8, 10, 12, 14, 16, 18, 20, 22, 24;
2, 4, 6, 8, 10, 12, 14, 16, 18, 20, 22, 24

Page 23 Groups of two
1 20 2 12 3 10 4 22 5 14 6 24 7 18 8 8 9 16 10 6 11 4

Page 24 Groups of three
A 6, 36, 21, 27, 18, 30, 15, 24, 9, 12, 33, 3
B 3, 6, 9, 12, 15, 18, 21, 24, 27, 30, 33, 36

Page 25 Groups of three
1 18 2 30 3 27 4 36 5 33 6 15 7 21 8 12 9 24 10 9 11 6

Page 26 Groups of four
A 8, 44, 28, 48, 24, 12, 40, 16, 36, 4, 20, 32
B 4, 8, 12, 16, 20, 24, 28, 32, 36, 40, 44, 48

Page 27 Groups of four
1 24 2 20 3 48 4 40 5 32 6 28 7 16 8 12 9 44 10 36 11 8

Page 28 Groups of five
A 20, 30, 50, 15, 45, 5, 60, 10, 35, 55, 40, 25
B 5, 10, 15, 20, 25, 30, 35, 40, 45, 50, 55, 60
5, 10, 15, 20, 25, 30, 35, 40, 45, 50, 55, 60

Page 29 Groups of five
1 60 **2** 20 **3** 35 **4** 55 **5** 25 **6** 50 **7** 30 **8** 45 **9** 15 **10** 40 **11** 10

Page 30 Groups of six
A 60, 30, 72, 6, 18, 66, 12, 36, 48, 24, 54, 42
B 6, 12, 18, 24, 30, 36, 42, 48, 54, 60, 66, 72

Page 31 Groups of six
1 36 **2** 18 **3** 72 **4** 12 **5** 60 **6** 42 **7** 30 **8** 54 **9** 24 **10** 66 **11** 48

Page 32 Dividing by two
A 1 6 **2** 4 **3** 12 **4** 3 **5** 10 **6** 11 **7** 2 **8** 9 **9** 8 **10** 5 **11** 1 **12** 7
B 3, 1, 10;   8, 7, 6;   9, 12, 4;   5, 2, 11

Page 33 Dividing by three
A 1 12 **2** 3 **3** 4 **4** 8 **5** 10 **6** 1 **7** 6 **8** 9 **9** 7 **10** 11 **11** 2 **12** 5
B 12, 3, 1;   11, 10, 6;   5, 9, 8;   4, 2, 7

Page 34 Dividing by four
A 1 9 **2** 4 **3** 2 **4** 12 **5** 6 **6** 8 **7** 5 **8** 7 **9** 10 **10** 11 **11** 3 **12** 1
B 1, 5, 6;   3, 9, 10;   7, 4, 12;   11, 2, 8

Page 35 Dividing by five
A 1 1 **2** 7 **3** 3 **4** 12 **5** 6 **6** 11 **7** 2 **8** 8 **9** 10 **10** 5 **11** 9 **12** 4
B 12, 6, 2;   3, 7, 8;   1, 11, 10;   9, 4, 5

Page 36 Dividing by six
A 1 3 **2** 8 **3** 5 **4** 7 **5** 11 **6** 10 **7** 9 **8** 1 **9** 6 **10** 4 **11** 12 **12** 2
B 11, 8, 5;   2, 1, 12;   9, 4, 3;   10, 7, 6

Page 37 Division with remainders
A 1 2 r 1, 5 r 3, 10 r 1, 9 r 2, 5 r 2, 3 r 3, 11 r 3, 7 r 1
2 11 r 1, 10, 8 r 1, 6 r 1, 3 r 1, 8, 9 r 1, 10 r 1
3 11 r 2, 9 r 1, 8 r 1, 5 r 2, 10 r 2, 7 r 1, 5 r 1, 6 r 2
4 11 r 4, 6 r 4, 3 r 3, 11 r 3, 4 r 1, 8 r 4, 7 r 4, 1 r 4
5 4 r 4, 10 r 3, 7 r 3, 5 r 2, 9 r 4, 2 r 5, 8 r 3, 11 r 5
B 1 11 r 1, 7 r 2, 5 r 3, 4 r 3, 3 r 5   **2** 7 r 0, 4 r 2, 3 r 2, 2 r 4, 2 r 2
3 10 r 1, 7 r 0, 5 r 1, 4 r 1, 3 r 3   **4** 9 r 1, 6 r 1, 4 r 3, 3 r 4, 3 r 1

Page 38 How much?
1 10p **2** 6p **3** 7p;   **4** 6p **5** 9p **6** 4p;   **7** 10p **8** 3p **9** 5p;   **10** 9p **11** 8p **12** 2p

Page 39 How much?
1 10p **2** 9p **3** 10p **4** 10p **5** 3p **6** 8p **7** 7p **8** 5p **9** 8p **10** 5p **11** 6p **12** 5p **13** 5p
14 9p **15** 9p **16** 10p **17** 10p **18** 9p **19** 7p **20** 7p **21** 4p **22** 8p **23** 8p **24** 4p

Page 40 How much?
1 8p **2** 13p **3** 10p **4** 11p **5** 18p **6** 16p **7** 18p **8** 17p **9** 7p **10** 15p **11** 15p **12** 20p
13 19p **14** 14p **15** 20p **16** 13p **17** 14p **18** 9p **19** 19p **20** 7p **21** 12p **22** 6p **23** 9p
24 15p

Page 41 Using 1p, 2p and 5p coins
A Check your child's answers total 16p, 20p, 18p and 19p.
B 1 2p, 2p **2** 5p, 2p **3** 5p, 1p **4** 2p, 1p **5** 5p, 5p
C 1 5p, 2p, 2p **2** 5p, 2p, 1p **3** 2p, 2p, 1p **4** 5p, 5p, 1p **5** 5p, 5p, 5p
D 1 4 x 5p **2** 5p, 5p, 5p, 1p **3** 2p, 2p, 2p, 1p **4** 5p, 5p, 2p, 1p **5** 5p, 5p, 2p, 2p;
6 5p, 2p, 2p, 1p **7** 5p, 5p, 5p, 2p **8** 4 x 2p **9** 5p, 5p, 1p, 1p **10** 5p, 2p, 1p, 1p
E 1 5p, 5p, 5p, 1p, 1p **2** 5p, 5p, 5p, 2p 2p **3** 5p, 5p, 2p, 1p, 1p **4** 5p, 2p, 1p, 1p, 1p
5 5p, 5p, 5p, 2p, 1p

Page 42 Making 10p
A 1 2p **2** 1p **3** 1p **4** 5p **5** 2p **6** 2p **7** 5p **8** 2p **9** 1p **10** 5p
B 1 3p – 3 x 1p or 2p, 1p **2** 4p – 2p, 2p or 1p, 1p, 2p **3** 2p **4** 1p;
5 4p – 2p, 2p (or equivalent) **6** 4p – 2p, 2p (or equivalent) **7** 3p – 3 x 1p, or 2p, 1p
8 4p – 2p, 2p (or equivalent)

Page 43 Shopping with 10p
1 5p **2** 7p **3** 7p **4** 2p **5** 5p **6** 7p **7** 4p **8** 3p **9** 8p **10** 4p **11** 5p **12** 4p **13** 6p **14** 6p
15 6p **16** 5p **17** 5p **18** 8p

Page 44 Addition to 10p
A 1 9p **2** 7p **3** 10p **4** 9p **5** 8p **6** 7p **7** 9p **8** 8p
B 1 6p **2** 7p **3** 9p **4** 3p **5** 5p **6** 6p **7** 4p **8** 9p

Page 45 Change from 5p
1 2p **2** 1p **3** 0p **4** 3p **5** 4p **6** 2p **7** 3p **8** 4p **9** 2p **10** 2p **11** 0p **12** 0p

Page 46 Change from 10p
A 1 1p **2** 3p **3** 2p **4** 1p **5** 5p **6** 4p **7** 2p **8** 1p **9** 5p **10** 6p **11** 1p **12** 1p
B 1 1p **2** 3 x 1p or 2p + 1p **3** 2p (or equivalent) **4** 1p **5** 5p (or equivalent)
6 2p + 2p (or equivalent) **7** 2p (or equivalent) **8** 1p **9** 5p (or equivalent)
10 3 x 2p (or equivalent) **11** 1p **12** 1p

Page 47 How much?
1 20p **2** 20p **3** 19p **4** 19p **5** 16p **6** 17p **7** 15p **8** 18p **9** 17p **10** 13p **11** 18p **12** 15p

Page 48 Using 10p, 5p, 2p and 1p coins
A 1 5p, 2p **2** 2p, 1p **3** 10p, 5p, 2p, 2p **4** 10p, 2p, 1p;
5 10p **6** 10p, 5p **7** 5p, 2p, 2p **8** 10p, 5p, 1p;
9 10p, 2p **10** 10p, 5p, 2p, 1p **11** 10p, 1p **12** 5p, 2p, 1p;
13 5p, 1p **14** 10p, 2p, 2p **15** 10p, 5p, 2p **16** 2p, 2p
B 3 coins 1 5p, 5p, 1p **2** 10p, 5p, 1p **3** 10p, 1p, 1p **4** 5p, 5p, 5p **5** 10p, 5p, 2p
6 10p, 2p, 1p
4 coins 1 10p, 2p, 2p, 2p **2** 10p, 2p, 2p, 1p **3** 10p, 5p, 2p, 2p **4** 10p, 2p, 1p, 1p
5 5p, 5p, 1p, 1p **6** 10p, 5p, 2p, 1p
5 coins 1 10p, 5p, 1p, 1p, 2p **2** 10p, 5p, 1p, 1p, 1p **3** 10p, 2p, 1p, 1p, 1p

4 10p, 2p, 2p, 2p, 1p **5** 5p, 5p, 2p, 1p, 1p **6** 10p, 2p, 2p, 1p, 1p
C 1 10p, 2p (or equivalent) **2** 5p, 2p (or equivalent) **3** 10p, 2p, 2p **4** 10p, 1p
5 10p, 5p, 2p, 1p **6** 5p, 2p, 2p; **7** 10p, 5p **8** 5p, 5p **9** 10p, 2p, 1p **10** 10p, 5p, 2p
11 5p, 2p, 1p **12** 10p, 5p, 1p

Page 49 Values up to 20p

1 5p **2** 2p **3** 2p **4** 5p **5** 1p **6** 10p **7** 5p **8** 2p **9** 5p **10** 1p **11** 1p **12** 2p

Page 50 Values up to 20p

A 1 3p **2** 6p **3** 1p **4** 4p **5** 4p **6** 8p **7** 9p **8** 7p **9** 5p **10** 12p **11** 12p **12** 11p
B 1 5p **2** 8p **3** 4p **4** 3p **5** 7p **6** 16p **7** 9p
8 1p **9** 6p **10** 10p **11** 13p **12** 11p **13** 2p **14** 14p

Page 51 Shopping with 15p

A soldier 8p; 7p; 5p, 2p **ball** 11p; 4p; 2p, 2p **comb** 14p; 1p; 1p
whistle 7p; 8p; 5p, 2p, 1p **doll's brush** 12p; 3p; 2p, 1p **toy watch** 12p; 3p; 2p, 1p
bracelet 13p; 2p; 2p **tank** 10p; 5p; 5p **car** 14p; 1p; 1p **toy ring** 9p; 6p; 5p, 1p
B Check that your child has drawn the correct coins, e.g.
1 10p **2** 5p, 2p, 2p **3** 10p, 2p, 1p **4** 10p, 2p **5** 10p, 2p **6** 10p, 1p **7** 10p, 2p, 2p
8 5p, 2p **9** 5p, 2p, 1p **10** 10p, 2p, 2p

Page 52 Shopping with 20p

A van 14p; 6p; 5p, 1p **fire-engine** 17p; 3p; 2p, 1p **police car** 16p; 4p; 2p, 2p
lorry 16p; 4p; 2p, 2p **bus** 19p; 1p; 1p **coach** 18p; 2p; 2p **saloon** 15p; 5p; 5p
racing car 15p; 5p; 5p
B racing car 10p, 5p **police car** 10p, 5p, 1p **van** 10p, 2p, 2p **coach** 10p, 5p, 2p, 1p
bus 10p, 5p, 2p, 2p **saloon** 10p, 5p **lorry** 10p, 5p, 1p **fire-engine** 10p, 5p, 2p

Page 53 Shopping with 15p

A 7p + 5p = 12p; 3p   5p + 6p = 11p; 4p   7p + 4p = 11p; 4p   7p + 6p = 13p; 2p
3p + 6p = 9p; 6p   7p + 5p = 12p; 3p   5p + 6p = 11p; 4p   6p + 7p = 13p; 2p
7p + 6p = 13p; 2p   4p + 3p = 7p; 8p   7p + 4p = 11p; 4p   5p + 6p = 11p; 4p
6p + 3p = 9p; 6p   7p + 6p = 13p; 2p   7p + 5p = 12p; 3p
B 1 1p **2** 2p, 1p **3** 5p, 1p **4** 5p **5** 2p, 2p

Page 54 Shopping with 20p

8p + 7p = 15p; 5p   8p + 9p = 17p; 3p   5p + 6p = 11p; 9p   7p + 9p = 16p; 4p
9p + 6p = 15p; 5p   7p + 7p = 14p; 6p   8p + 6p = 14p; 6p   6p + 8p = 14p; 6p
9p + 9p = 18p; 2p   9p + 5p = 14p; 6p   9p + 6p = 15p; 5p   8p + 7p = 15p; 5p
9p + 8p = 17p; 3p   6p + 5p = 11p; 9p   7p + 9p = 16p; 4p   6p + 9p = 15p; 5p
8p + 8p = 16p; 4p   6p + 9p = 15p; 5p   9p + 7p = 16p; 4p   5p + 7p = 12p; 8p

Page 55 The cake shop

A 4p; 3 x 4p = 12p; 3p   4p; 2 x 4p = 8p; 7p   2p; 2 x 2p = 4p; 11p
4p; 2 x 4p = 8p; 7p   3p; 3 x 3p = 9p; 6p   1p; 2 x 1p = 2p; 13p   1p; 4 x 1p = 4p; 11p
1p; 5 x 1p = 5p; 10p   5p; 3 x 5p = 15p; 0   4p; 3 x 4p = 12p; 3p
5p; 2 x 5p = 10p; 5p   2p; 4 x 2p = 8p; 7p   1p; 7 x 1p = 7p; 8p   1p; 9 x 1p = 9p; 6p
3p; 5 x 3p = 15p; 0   4p; 2 x 4p = 8p; 7p   4p; 3 x 4p = 12p; 3p
B 1 15 **2** 3 **3** 3;   **4** 5 **5** 15 **6** 15

Page 56 The sweet shop

6p; 3 x 6p = 18p; 2p	9p; 2 x 9p = 18p; 2p	5p; 2 x 5p = 10p; 10p
6p; 3 x 6p = 18p; 2p	5p; 3 x 5p = 15p; 5p	4p; 2 x 4p = 8p; 12p
7p; 2 x 7p = 14p; 6p	6p; 2 x 6p = 12p; 8p	5p; 3 x 5p = 15p; 5p
6p; 2 x 6p = 12p; 8p	5p; 2 x 5p = 10p; 10p	6p; 3 x 6p = 18p; 2p
5p; 4 x 5p = 20p; 0	5p; 2 x 5p = 10p; 10p	4p; 4 x 4p = 16p; 4p
6p; 2 x 6p = 12p; 8p	4p; 3 x 4p = 12p; 8p	5p; 3 x 5p = 15p; 5p
5p; 4 x 5p = 20p; 0	4p; 5 x 4p = 20p; 0	5p; 4 x 5p = 20p; 0

Page 57 Time — o'clock
A 3, 7, 4, 12; 1, 8, 10, 6; 5, 9, 11, 2
B Check that your child has drawn the correct times.

Page 58 Time — half past
A 6, 1, 8, 9; 2, 7, 12, 4; 5, 11, 3, 10
B Check that your child has drawn the correct times.

Page 59 Time — quarter past
A 4, 11, 7, 10; 9, 2, 8, 5; 3, 6, 12, 1
B Check that your child has correctly drawn the stated times.

Page 60 Time — quarter to
A 1, 8, 9, 5; 7, 11, 4, 10; 2, 3, 12, 6
B Check that your child has correctly drawn the stated times.

Page 61 The calendar
1 Monday, Thursday, Thursday, Friday, Wednesday;
Monday, Saturday, Tuesday, Monday, Wednesday
2 Monday
3 Wednesday
4 4
5 Wednesdays
6 5
7 4th, 11th, 18th, 25th
8 2nd, 9th, 16th, 23rd, 30th
9 7
10 7

Page 62 Length
A 1 B **2** B **3** longest B, shortest C **4** shortest B, longest C
B 1 3cm **2** 4cm **3** 7cm **4** 5cm **5** 12cm

Page 63 Mass
A 1 500 g **2** 1 kg **3** 500 g **4** 250 g **5** 250 g **6** 250 g **7** 250 g **8** 500 g
B 4, 6, 8, 10, 20; 4, 8, 12, 16, 20

Page 64 Graphs — pictograms
A 1 4 **2** 6 **3** 7 **4** 5 **5** 22
B 1 5 **2** 4 **3** 7 **4** 6 **5** 9